Contemporary Scenes for Actors
Women

Michael Earley was Chief Producer of Plays for BBC Radio Drama in London. He was Chairman of the Theatre Studies Program at Yale University and taught acting, dramatic literature and playwriting there and at New York University's Tisch School of the Arts, the Juilliard School's Acting Program, Smith College and various other schools and universities in America and Britain. He is publisher of Methuen Drama.

Philippa Keil has edited seven books for Methuen including *Contemporary Scenes for Actors* (Men), *The Contemporary Monologue* (Women and Men), *The Modern Monologue* (Women and Men) and *The Classical Monologue* (Women and Men). She is also a freelance writer, editor and translator who trained at the Yale School of Drama. She graduated from Sussex University where she acted, directed and produced plays for the Frontdoor Theatre, and then worked professionally in London at Richmond's Orange Tree Theatre and in America with her own company Ballet Cirque.

by the same authors

Contemporary Scenes for Actors (Men)
The Contemporary Monologue (Women and Men)
The Modern Monologue (Women and Men)
The Classical Monologue (Women and Men)
Soliloquy! The Shakespeare Monologues (Women and Men)
Solo: The Best Monologues of the 8os (Women and Men)

Contemporary Scenes for Actors
Women

Edited with notes and commentaries by

MICHAEL EARLEY
& PHILIPPA KEIL

Routledge/Theatre Arts Books
New York

1 3 5 7 9 10 8 6 4 2

First published in the United Kingdom in 1999 by
Methuen Publishing Limited

Published in the USA and Canada by
Routledge/Theatre Arts Books
29 West 35th Street
New York, NY 10001
www.routledge–ny.com

Copyright in the selections, format, introductions and commentaries © 1999
Michael Earley and Philippa Keil.

A CIP catalogue record for this book is available from the Library of
Congress

ISBN 0 878 30078 3

Typeset by Deltatype Ltd, Birkenhead, Merseyside

Printed and bound in Great Britain by
Cox & Wyman Ltd, Reading, Berks

CAUTION

Contents

Notes to the Actors

This book of scenes, arranged specifically for actors who are working together, offers a selection of pieces from some of the most energetic and exciting plays of the past few years. As we enter the new millennium, the contemporary theatre has suddenly revitalised itself and is attracting a whole new generation of young dramatists who are capturing the imagination of performers and audiences on both sides of the Atlantic. These writers are producing muscular, compelling and often controversial plays which are finding favour in both the commercial and subsidised theatres. These dramas, often set against a backdrop of urban ennui and violence, share common chords of disaffection, anger and angst. The dramatic tones of these works vary from the bleaky tragic to the openly farcical, offering a rich range of parts into which actors can really sink their teeth.

The scenes in this volume provide a representative cross-section from a whole range of recent British, American and Irish plays. We have applied strict criteria in our selection process so that we could give actors all-round scenes, which will work in the classroom, audition room or rehearsal studio. Professional actors have proved in performance every one of the plays from which we have chosen material. Some have had further productions since their premieres. They also work as pieces of writing independent of a particular performance and performers. Since all of the plays from which the scenes are derived are in print, we cannot stress too strongly the importance of reading and being familiar with the whole play before you begin work. In fact, you must work through the play as often as possible to gain the full context of both the characters and their dramatic situation. Scenes provide links between a play's key stages. The actor must know where the character is coming from and where the character is heading towards before making complete sense of a character's journey through the play. Something in the first or last part of a script may hold a vital clue for understanding the scene on which you are working. So connect your scene to others as you work.

We have also selected scenes which we think work because each, in their own way, is a mini-drama with its own beginning, middle and end. This is a crucial feature of any good scene. In performing the material it helps when you can actually follow a single arc of action or sequence of events which appear to have an independent life from the rest of the play. All the information and details given to the actors about the characters create a story which then integrates with the other stories told in the play. We judge a play by the way its various plot strands either confirm or contradict the knowledge we receive scene by scene. The tension that results from this rich interplay of narrative results in drama.

We have tried to ensure that each of the characters has an equal stake in the scene. In some instances a character's silent presence and unspoken reactions offer an acting challenge equal to that of a verbal character. Not every character needs to speak volumes in order to hold the stage.

In thinking about his or her character, the actor can come to the task with a whole range of questions that can allow you to uncover a wealth of details embedded in the text. The following are but a few simple suggestions to help you begin this uncovering process for yourself:

- *Who am I?* The big question which this scene might only partly answer. The rest of the play, however, will shed further light. Be careful, however, of information which might lead to self-delusion or give you a false sense of self.
- *What do I want?* In every scene the character is trying to achieve something, to get something from another character on-stage. As characters play against each other they can throw up obstacles which need to be deflected. How to deal with these obstacles is part of the acting challenge.
- *What is my status?* This can often be a key question when trying to get inside a character. Characters are often matched or mismatched according to their status in life: masters and

servants, parents and children, men and women, etc. The chemistry between characters often starts with this basic question.

- *How articulate am I?* This is a useful question to ask especially where text is concerned. We are what we speak, and you can often pursue a rich exploration of character by looking at the kind of language they use. Some characters have a fluid ease with words but may use them as a mask. Other characters may be verging on the inarticulate, but use the few words they possess with unusual power and passion.
- *How well do we work together?* This is a crucial question for both actors working on a scene together. It can often lead directly to uncovering the dynamics which propel a scene. Are you friends or enemies? Do you love or hate each other? Are you trying to help or deny one another? You can ask an endless series of simple and more complicated questions like these in order to delve deeper and deeper into the on-stage relationship.

As actors you should prepare your own agenda of further questions in order to explore not only your own character but also the nature of your on-stage relationship with your partner.

So much about scene work is wrestling with the qualities offered by a two-character scene. Unlike a monologue, where you are acting alone on-stage and project outwards to an audience, in a scene the acting energy is far less presentational and more concentrated on a relationship. You have to learn to act together, not separately. Actors in a scene make a pact to work in concert, even when the scene seems to be pulling time apart. You search the script together for collaborative cues which allow each of you to pick up from one another and pass the baton back and forth. A scene can often be like a relay race. You will begin to notice that timing and rhythm – how you play together back and forth – begin to enter into the process. The more knowledge each of you shares about the scene the better the job you'll perform together.

We have designed this volume to work in tandem with *Contemporary Scenes for Actors: Men*. The introductions for each scene provide the basic set-up and character information to launch you into the specific action. Each scene is then followed by a commentary, which is not intended as acting or director's notes but is meant to highlight some useful features and details in the scene. But the actors must do the real work of asking the important questions and uncovering any scene's dynamic for themselves. Clearly this will change with each new pairing of actors. We want to stress again that there can be no substitute for reading the entire play. Without doing so you risk only getting a piece of the action, a part of the story, a selected view of the characters. Any scene can only be a part of the whole. The Play Sources will direct you to the full version of each text.

Michael Earley
Philippa Keil
London 1999

Scenes for One Woman and One Man

The Beauty Queen of Leenane
Martin McDonagh

Act I, scene 3. The living-room kitchen of a rural cottage in the west of Ireland. Night. Set only just illuminated by the orange coals through the bars of the range. Radio has been left on low in the kitchen. (NB The scene preceding this one can be found on page 108 of this volume.)

Maureen Folan is 'a plain, slim woman of about forty' and Pato Dooley is 'a good-looking man, aged about forty'. He has been working as a casual labourer on building sites in England and has come back to Ireland for a brief visit to 'say hello and goodbye' to his 'Yankee' relatives. Maureen lives at home with Mag, her aged hypochondriac mother, tending their isolated small holding. These two women co-exist in a constant state of hate, resentment and bitterness. The harsh loneliness of their poor rural surroundings has an inexorable influence over their lives. At the age of twenty-five, while working as a cleaner, Maureen had a nervous breakdown. Mag's response to this, as she never fails to remind Maureen, was to have her put away in a 'nut-house' for a month. In this scene, Maureen is bringing Pato home late in the evening after a party for his American relatives. This is the first time we see these two characters together. They have known one another since they were children but have never been romantically involved. As the scene starts 'footsteps and voices of Maureen and Pato are heard outside, both slightly drunk'.

PATO (*off, singing*). 'The Cadillac stood by the house . . .'
MAUREEN (*off*). Shh, Pato . . .
PATO (*off. Singing quietly*). 'And the Yanks they were within.' (*Speaking.*) What was it that oul fella used to say, now?

MAUREEN (*off*). What oul fella, now?

(MAUREEN *opens the door and the two of them enter, turning the lights on. MAUREEN is in a new black dress, cut quite short. PATO is a good-looking man of about the same age as her.*)

PATO. The oul fella who used to chase oul whatyoucall. Oul Bugs Bunny.

MAUREEN. Would you like a cup of tea, Pato?

PATO. I would.

(MAUREEN *switches the kettle on.*)

MAUREEN. Except keep your voice down, now.

PATO (*quietly*). I will, I will. (*Pause.*) I can't remember *what* he used to say. The oul fella used to chase Bugs Bunny. It was something, now.

MAUREEN. Look at this. The radio left on too, the daft oul bitch.

PATO. Sure, what harm? No, leave it on, now. It'll cover up the sounds.

MAUREEN. What sounds?

PATO. The smooching sounds.

(*He gently pulls her to him and they kiss a long while, then stop and look at each other. The kettle has boiled. MAUREEN gently breaks away, smiling, and starts making the tea.*)

MAUREEN. Will you have a biscuit with your tea?

PATO. I will. What biscuits do you have, now?

MAUREEN. Em, only Kimberleys.

PATO. I'll leave it so, Maureen. I do hate Kimberleys. In fact I think Kimberleys are the most horrible biscuits in the world.

MAUREEN. The same as that, I hate Kimberleys. I only get them to torment me mother.

PATO. I can't see why the Kimberley people go making them at all. Coleman Connor ate a whole pack of Kimberleys one time and he was sick for a week. (*Pause.*) Or was it Mikados? It was some kind of horrible biscuits.

4

She does have a creepy oul voice. Always scared
song did when I was a lad. She's like a ghoul
(*Pause.*) Does the grandmother die at the end,
is she just sleeping?

...EN. Just sleeping, I think she is.

...Aye ...

...EN (*pause*). While the two go hand in hand
the fields.

...Aye.

...EN. Be moonlight.

...*ods*). They don't write songs like that any more.

...hrist. (MAUREEN *laughs. Brighter.*) Wasn't it a
...t though, Maureen, now?

...EN. It was.

...idn't we send them on their way well?

...N. We did, we did.

...t a dry eye.

...N. Indeed.

...N. Indeed.

...That we did. That we did.

...(*pause*). So who *was* the Yankee girl you did
...ands all over?

...*hing*). Oh will you stop it with your 'hands all
...y touched her, I did.

...Oh-ho!

...cond cousin of me uncle, I think she is.
...body. Healey or Hooley. Healey. Boston,

...That was illegal so if it's your second cousin

...me arse, and it's not *my* second cousin she
...l what's so illegal? Your second cousin's
...t of bounds, are they?

...hey are!

MAUREEN. Is it true Coleman cut the ears off Valene's
dog and keeps them in his room in a bag?

PATO. He showed me them ears one day.

MAUREEN. That's awful spiteful, cutting the ears off a
dog.

PATO. It *is* awful spiteful.

MAUREEN. It would be spiteful enough to cut the ears
off anybody's dog, let alone your own brother's dog.

PATO. And it had seemed a nice dog.

MAUREEN. Aye. (*Pause.*) Aye.

(*Awkward pause.* PATO *cuddles up behind her.*)

PATO. You feel nice to be giving a squeeze to.

MAUREEN. Do I?

PATO. Very nice.

(MAUREEN *continues making the tea as* PATO *holds her.
A little embarrassed and awkward, he breaks away from her
after a second and idles a few feet away.*)

MAUREEN. Be sitting down for yourself, now, Pato.

PATO. I will. (*Sits at table.*) I do do what I'm told, I do.

MAUREEN. Oh-ho, do you now? That's the first time
tonight I did notice. Them stray oul hands of yours.

PATO. Sure, I have no control over me hands. They have
a mind of their own. (*Pause.*) Except I didn't notice you
complaining overmuch anyways, me stray oul hands. Not
too many complaints at all!

MAUREEN. I had complaints when they were straying
over that Yank girl earlier on in the evening.

PATO. Well, I hadn't noticed you there at that time,
Maureen. How was I to know the beauty queen of
Leenane was still yet to arrive?

MAUREEN. 'The beauty queen of Leenane.' Get away
with ya!

PATO. Is true!

MAUREEN. Why so have no more than two words
passed between us the past twenty year?

5

PATO. Sure, it's took me all this time to get up the courage.

MAUREEN (smiling). Ah, bollocks to ya!

(PATO smiles. MAUREEN brings the tea over and sits down.)

PATO. I don't know, Maureen. I don't know.

MAUREEN. Don't know what?

PATO. Why I never got around to really speaking to you or asking you out or the like. I don't know. Of course, hopping across to that bastarding oul place every couple of months couldn't've helped.

MAUREEN. England? Aye. Do you not like it there so?

PATO (pause). It's money. (Pause.) And it's Tuesday I'll be back there again.

MAUREEN. Tuesday? This Tuesday?

PATO. Aye. (Pause.) It was only to see the Yanks off I was over. To say hello and say goodbye. No time back at all.

MAUREEN. That's Ireland, anyways. There's always someone leaving.

PATO. It's always the way.

MAUREEN. Bad, too.

PATO. What can you do?

MAUREEN. Stay?

PATO (pause). I do ask meself, if there was good work in Leenane, would I stay in Leenane? I mean, there never will be good work, but hypothetically, I'm saying. Or even bad work. Any work. And when I'm over there in London and working in rain and it's more or less cattle I am, and the young fellas cursing over cards and drunk and sick, and the oul digs over there, all pee-stained mattresses and nothing to do but watch the clock . . . when it's there I am, it's here I wish I was, of course. Who wouldn't? But when it's here I am . . . it isn't *there* I want to be, of course not. But I know it isn't here I want to be either.

6

MAUREEN. And why, Pato?

PATO. I can't put my finger on it's beautiful here, a fool can see. green, and people speak. But everybody else's business . . . I can't kick a cow in Leenane with a grudge twenty year.

MAUREEN. It's true enough

PATO. It is. In England they and it's funny but that isn't sometimes it is . . . ah, I don

MAUREEN (pause). Do you in the one place so, Pato suppose.

PATO (half-laughing). 'W

MAUREEN. You will som Wouldn't you want to?

PATO. I can't say it's s over.

MAUREEN. Of course stashed all over, you w

PATO (smiling). I have

MAUREEN. You hav

PATO. I may have on to, now.

MAUREEN. Hello r

PATO. Is true. (Pau

MAUREEN (pause)

(Pause. PATO shrug Pause. The song " Murphy, has just st

MAUREEN (cont song. Oul Delia M

PATO. This is a

MAUREEN. It

8

PATO me thi singing now, o

MAUR

PATO.

MAUR through

PATO.

MAURE

PATO (Thank Cl grand nig

MAURE

PATO. D

MAUREE

PATO. N

MAUREE

PATO. Eh

MAUREE

PATO. Ay

MAUREE have your h

PATO (laug over'?! Barel

MAUREEN

PATO. A s Dolores some too, she lives

MAUREEN she is.

PATO. Illegal is anyway, an boobs aren't o

MAUREEN. T

8

PATO. I don't know about that. I'll have to consult with me lawyer on that one. I may get arrested the next time. And I have a defence anyways. She had dropped some Taytos on her blouse, there, I was just brushing them off for her.

MAUREEN. Taytos me arsehole, Pato Dooley!

PATO. Is true! (*Lustful pause. Nervously.*) Like this is all it was . . .

(PATO *slowly reaches out and gently brushes at, then gradually fondles,* MAUREEN*'s breasts. She caresses his hand as he's doing so, then slowly gets up and sits across his lap, fondling his head as he continues touching her.*)

MAUREEN. She was prettier than me.

PATO. You're pretty.

MAUREEN. She was prettier.

PATO. I like you.

MAUREEN. You have blue eyes.

PATO. I do.

MAUREEN. Stay with me tonight.

PATO. I don't know, now, Maureen.

MAUREEN. Stay. Just tonight.

PATO (*pause*). Is your mother asleep?

MAUREEN. I don't care if she is or she isn't. (*Pause.*) Go lower.

(PATO *begins easing his hands down her front.*)

Go lower . . . Lower . . .

(*His hands reach her crotch. She tilts her head back slightly. The song on the radio ends. Blackout.*)

COMMENTARY: Notice how unromantic the setting is; the offer of tea and 'Kimberleys' is not exactly the food of love. Mag is asleep upstairs, although she could well be awake and eavesdropping. The radio is randomly playing in the background to cover up the 'smooching sounds'. Both Maureen and Pato have come back with the same idea in mind, although they obviously have not talked about it. She wants him and he wants her but there is a preliminary wariness to be articulated first. Maureen appears to have the upper hand; to be controlling the situation, gently insinuating that Pato has taken his time in making his moves on her. She jealously reminds Pato of his earlier attentions towards the Yankee girl, but her harping on this subject could almost lose her Pato altogether. Maureen puts Pato in a position where he feels compelled to explain himself. Considering her relatively protected life and her lack of boyfriends – 'What have I ever done but *kissed* two men the past forty year' – she is remarkably confident with Pato. This is almost the reverse of the situation we would expect. Pato is certainly lustful, but is hampered by his tongue-tied shyness when challenged by Maureen's confident taunting wit. He is tenative and she knows just what she wants. He will deflect this with his talk about biscuits and assorted chit-chat. To help your performances you must decide just how experienced and confident these characters are in love and sex.

Boys' Life
Howard Korder

Act 1, scene 2. A large city. The present. A child's bedroom. Phil and Karen standing at opposite ends of the room, facing each other. The bed is piled with coats. Sounds of a party filter in from outside.

Phil (late 20s) works at a 9-to-5 job. He's neurotic and a hypochondriac. Phil has a dismal track record in his relationships with women, and his friends are used to hearing his 'sexual sob stories'. Finding a girlfriend has become an obsession for Phil. Karen (late 20s) is also neurotic and has a very low sense of self-esteem. Later in the play it is revealed that 'She says she's frigid . . . She says her uncle raped her when she was ten.' Unlike Phil, Karen is afraid of relationships and commitment. Several months ago this unlikely couple had a brief, two-night fling. In this scene they meet again for the first time.

PHIL. Well, there *you* are.

KAREN. Yes.

PHIL. And here I am.

KAREN. Yes.

PHIL. So here we are, both of us. Together.

KAREN. Talking.

PHIL. Right here in the same room.

KAREN. It's pretty amazing. (*Pause.*) Enjoying the party?

PHIL. Oh yes. Certainly. Yes yes yes.

KAREN. Mmmm.

PHIL. No.

KAREN. Oh.

PHIL. Not in the larger sense.

KAREN. Why did you come?

PHIL. I was invited. I mean . . . Jack invited me.

KAREN. And you do everything Jack says.

PHIL. No, I . . . he's my friend. My oldest friend. (*Pause.*) You look great tonight, Karen.

KAREN. Thanks.

PHIL. No, I mean it. Just wonderful. (*Pause.*)

KAREN. You look good.

PHIL. No.

KAREN. You do.

PHIL. No I don't.

KAREN. Really, you do.

PHIL. Do I?

KAREN. What do you want, Phil?

PHIL. Well, I don't *want* anything. I just wanted to . . . say hello.

KAREN. Hello.

PHIL. Yes, well. (*Pause.*) That's lovely, what you have on, what is it?

KAREN. A dress.

PHIL. I've always admired your sense of humor, Karen.

KAREN. What do you want, Phil? [(*The door opens and a* MAN *pops his head in.*)

MAN. Oh. I'm sorry.

KAREN. We're almost done.

MAN. Oh. Well. Fine. I'll, ah . . . fine. (*He exits, closing the door.*)

PHIL. What was that all about?

KAREN. What?

PHIL. That. That guy.

KAREN. I don't know.

PHIL. Well, you seemed pretty familiar with him.]

KAREN. Are you feeling okay?

PHIL. Hmm? Oh, sure. Things are going really really great for me right now. Just fine. I have my own partition now, over at the office, they put up one of those, ah . . . so *that's* really good. And I'm going to the spa a lot, I'm working ou – well, I can't use the machines cause you know of my back, but I love the Jacuzzi, so, actually, it's strange, cause I fell asleep in it, in the whirlpool, and when I woke up I had this incredible headache, I mean it would *not* go away, I felt this thing here like the size of a peach pit, I went for a *blood* test, I was convinced I, you hear all this stuff now, the way it's spreading, I mean I'm not – but I was sure I had it.

KAREN. Had what?

PHIL. You know. (*Pause.*)

KAREN. And?

PHIL. I didn't. So. (*Pause.* KAREN *looks at the door.*) Anyway, it's funny we both happened to turn up here tonight, isn't it, cause I was just thinking. I was wondering . . . I mean, it's a couple of months since I last spoke to you and I was just *wondering* if we were still, you know, seeing each other.

KAREN. *Seeing* each other.

PHIL. Yes.

KAREN. No. (*Pause.*)

PHIL. All right.

KAREN. We were never seeing each other, Phil.

PHIL. Well, no, not actually *seeing* . . .

KAREN. We slept together once.

PHIL. Twice.

KAREN. You left before I woke up.

PHIL. Okay, yeah, but . . . I mean, *everybody* does that.

KAREN. And you never called.

PHIL. Now . . . now about *that*, you see, I was involved in a very bad kind of situation then, and I wasn't really in a position to, ah . . . as much as I *wanted* to . . . and I *did*, very, very –

KAREN. What do you want?

13

PHIL (*pause*). Well, I'd like another shot at it.

KAREN. At what?

PHIL. At you. To get to know you.

KAREN. I'm really not worth the effort, Phil.

PHIL. You're seeing someone else, right?

KAREN. That's got nothing to –

PHIL. You *are* seeing someone.

KAREN. Not actually *seeing* . . .

PHIL. No, no, it's fine. Early bird and all that stuff. I'm fine. Everything is fine.

KAREN. It's got nothing to do with you, Phil. There's just a lot of things I have to work through right now. But I like you, I do. You're . . . you're a wonderful person.

PHIL. You're a wonderful person too, Karen.

KAREN. Well, so are you, Phil.

PHIL. That's right. We both are. (*He hugs* KAREN.) Listen to this. A guy in my office has a cabin upstate. He never uses it. It's on the edge of a beautiful freshwater lake. Why don't we go there, just the two of us, we spend the weekend, relax, get out of the city . . . do some straight thinking. What do you say?

KAREN. No.

PHIL. Is it because of this guy you're seeing?

KAREN. Well, I'm not actually *seeing* –

PHIL. Then what is it?

KAREN. It's just not a good idea.

PHIL. It's not?

KAREN. No. Not at all. (*Pause.*) You're touching my breasts, Phil. [(*The* MAN *pops his head through the door.*)

MAN. Oh gosh. Beg pardon. (*He shuts the door.*)]

PHIL. I think about you a lot, Karen.

KAREN. You do.

PHIL. Yes. At work, you know, the laundromat, in the

shower . . . places like that. (*Pause.*) I mean that in the positive sense.

KAREN. I'm not worth the trouble.

PHIL. It's just two days out of your life, Karen. This could turn out to be something really special, it'll be over before you know it.

KAREN. You're making this very difficult.

PHIL. I'm making it incredibly *easy*. Come up to the country with me.

KAREN. Phil –

PHIL. Come.

KAREN. Please, Phil –

PHIL. I'm asking for a *chance*.

KAREN. Oh, no. Oh no. This is coming at a very bad time for me. I don't think I can handle this right now. My life is a real big mess, okay, and . . . I read that by the time you're five you've already developed the major patterns for the rest of your life. I mean whether you're going to be basically happy or . . . a fireman, a lesbian, whatever. And of course it's not fair at all, because nobody tells a little kid anything about that. But that's the way it is. So I've been thinking about this. And it occurs to me that somewhere along the line I screwed up really bad. I made a very poor choice about something and now there's nothing I can do to change it.

PHIL. I think I love you.

KAREN. You haven't even been listening.

PHIL. Of course I have. You were talking about your childhood, right? I love you.

KAREN. No, Phil. I'm really very flattered –

PHIL. I'm not saying it to flatter you, Karen. We're not talking about your drapes. We're talking about this very real and undeniable feeling I have for you. So you're not happy. I think I can sense that from what you just told me.

But *nobody's* happy. That's the way things are *supposed* to be. You think I'm happy? I'm not happy, I'm miserable.

KAREN. I am too.

PHIL. I know you are. That's why I feel so close to you. Karen? I can *make* you happy. And you can make me happy. We can help each other.

KAREN. You just said that nobody is happy.

PHIL. I didn't *mean* that. I feel so crazy when I'm with you I don't know what I'm saying. I love you.

KAREN. No – please –

PHIL. I love you. I'm sick with needing you. It's an actual disease. I'm all swollen and rotten inside, my brain is decomposing, and it's because of you.

KAREN. What's wrong with you, Phil?

PHIL. I'm dying without you, Karen. I'm serious. Has anyone ever told you anything like that? Ever?

KAREN. No. Never.

PHIL. Because no one has ever loved you as much as I do. Jesus, Karen, help me! [(*The* MAN *pops his head through the door.*)

MAN. Excuse me . . .

PHIL. What? What do you want?

MAN. Well . . . my coat . . .

PHIL. In a minute.

MAN. I've been waiting –

PHIL. GO AWAY! (*The* MAN *shuts the door.*)]
I love you.

KAREN. For how long?

PHIL. Until I'm in my grave. Longer. Forever.

KAREN. No, I mean . . . how long would we have to be away for?

PHIL. As long as you want. We don't even have to come back.

KAREN. I was thinking just the weekend.

PHIL. Yes, yes, the weekend. A day. An hour. A single second.

KAREN. I have pasta class Monday nights.

PHIL. Great. Fabulous. (*Pause.*)

KAREN. I wish I could, Phil. It's not that I don't want to . . .

PHIL. If you want to, just say yes. Don't worry about the rest.

KAREN. I can't.

PHIL. Then just say maybe.

KAREN. If I say maybe, you'll think I'm saying yes.

PHIL. I won't. I promise. I'm very clear on maybe. (*Pause.*) Please, Karen. Give me a crumb. Throw me a line.

KAREN. Oh, let me think about it. I have to . . . okay. Maybe. I'd like to – I don't know, maybe.

PHIL. Maybe. Maybe. Thank you, Karen. You won't be sorry. I'm crazy about you. You know that, don't you?

KAREN. I'm not worth it, Phil. Really.

PHIL. This is the happiest day of my life. (*He kisses her and eases her down onto the bed. He climbs on top of her and starts to caress her.* [*The* MAN *enters.*)

MAN. Look, I'm very sorry about this, but I need my coat.]

(KAREN *breaks away and sits on the edge of the bed.*)
[Sorry.

KAREN. That's all right. We're done.

MAN. Are you?]

PHIL (*rising from the bed*). Come on. Let's get back to the party.

KAREN. No, you go ahead.

PHIL. You're not coming?

KAREN. In a minute.

PHIL (*moving toward her*). Is everything okay?

KAREN. Yes, yes, it's really – Phil, no please, please, just stay away – [(*To the* MAN.) Look, I'm sorry, I – (*Turning away.*)] Oh God I hate myself so *much*! (*She runs out of the room.*)

PHIL (*following her*). Karen, wait a – (*She slams the door.*) Shit. Shit shit shit! (*He leans against the door. Silence.*)

COMMENTARY: The playwright gives the actors very few concrete facts about either character. It may help you to try and create your own histories for them. Although this is the only scene in which Karen actually appears, Phil's infatuation and obsession with her only increase, at first in this scene and then as the play progresses. Notice the extremely unromantic setting in which the two find themselves – a child's bedroom that is being used as a dumping place for coats. It is important not to let the scene become too serious. The passion and tragedy all have an oddball edge as their self-absorption becomes ever more absurd. Phil is a natural gabbler with a tendency to run at the mouth. Every time Phil tries to break the ice Karen responds with a quirky question or sardonic observation. Despite her obvious reluctance and reticence he blunders on with increasing desperation. The scene opens with them isolated on either side of the stage but fairly quickly Phil not only engineers a hug, but also starts fondling Karen's breasts. It is important for the actors to choreograph the pace of this comic seduction. They both over-analyse and interpret each other's words and actions. She is underwhelmed by his overwhelming propositions and flattery. Notice that with each brush off from Karen, Phil becomes ever more desperate and verbose.

Broken Glass
Arthur Miller

Act 1, scene 2. The Gellburg bedroom in a house in Brooklyn, New York. The last days of November 1938.

The Gellburgs, Sylvia (mid 40s) and Phillip (late 40s), have been married for over twenty years. For the past nine days she has been confined to a wheelchair suffering from a mysterious paralysis of her legs. She is a 'buxom, capable and warm woman. Right now her hair is brushed down to her shoulders, and she is in a nightgown and robe.' Soon after they were married their son Jerome was born. Following her son's birth Sylvia was eager to return to her job as a bookkeeper, but Phillip categorically refused to let her. By coincidence, at about the same time, Phillip suddenly became impotent. Over the years these two particular incidents have fuelled Sylvia's growing sense of resentment. She has maintained a passionate devotion to books, and has become increasingly obsessed with reading the papers for news of what is happening to the Jews in Nazi Germany. Phillip is a slender, intense man. 'He is in a black suit, black tie and shoes and white shirt.' Phillip works at the Brooklyn Guarantee and Trust, running their Mortgage Department. He is a workaholic, putting in ten or eleven hours a day at the office. Phillip is described as being an 'uptight little pisser'. He is proud of what he has achieved as a Jew in a predominantly gentile world, and yet 'he'd rather not be one'. This is not the happiest of marriages, and the absence of sex for the last twenty years due to Phillip's impotence has only aggravated things. Phillip is imbued with pent-up anger and a violent rage is kept just below the surface. As this scene starts Phillip returns home unexpectedly, following a secret consultation with Sylvia's doctor who has suggested that her illness may be due to a psychosomatic rather than a physical cause. Sylvia is reading a newspaper. 'Suddenly she turns in shock – Gellburg is standing behind her. He holds a small paper bag.'

19

SYLVIA. Oh! I didn't hear you come in.

GELLBURG. I tiptoed, in case you were dozing off . . . (*His dour smile.*) I bought you some sour pickles.

SYLVIA. Oh, that's nice! Later maybe. You have one.

GELLBURG. I'll wait. (*Awkwardly but determined.*) I was passing Greenberg's on Flatbush Avenue and I suddenly remembered how you used to love them. Remember?

SYLVIA. Thanks, that's nice of you. What were you doing on Flatbush Avenue?

GELLBURG. There's a property across from A&S. I'm probably going to foreclose.

SYLVIA. Oh that's sad. Are they nice people?

GELLBURG (*shrugs*). People are people – I gave them two extensions but they'll never manage . . . nothing up here. (*Taps his temple.*)

SYLVIA. Aren't you early?

GELLBURG. I got worried about you. Doctor come?

SYLVIA. He called; he has results of the tests but he wants to come tomorrow when he has more time to talk to me. He's really very nice.

GELLBURG. How was it today?

SYLVIA. I'm so sorry about this.

GELLBURG. You'll get better, don't worry about it. Oh! – there's a letter from the Captain. (*Takes letter out of his jacket pocket.*)

SYLVIA. Jerome?

GELLBURG (*terrific personal pride*). Read it. (*His purse-mouthed grin is intense.*) That's your son. General MacArthur talked to him twice.

SYLVIA. Fort Sill?

GELLBURG. Oklahoma. *He's going to lecture them on artillery!* In *Fort Sill*! That's the field artillery centre. (*She looks up dumbly.*) That's like being invited to the Vatican to lecture the Pope.

20

SYLVIA. Imagine. (*She folds the letter and hands it back to him.*)

GELLBURG (*restraining greater resentment*). I don't understand this attitude.

SYLVIA. Why? I'm happy for him.

GELLBURG. You don't seem happy to me.

SYLVIA. I'll never get used to it. Who goes in the Army? Men who can't do anything else.

GELLBURG. I wanted people to see that a Jew doesn't have to be a lawyer or a doctor or a businessman.

SYLVIA. That's fine, but why must it be Jerome?

GELLBURG. For a Jewish boy, West Point is an honour. Without Mr Case's connections, he'd never would have gotten in. He could be the first Jewish general in the United States Army. Doesn't it mean something to be his mother?

SYLVIA (*with an edge of resentment*). Well, I said I'm glad.

GELLBURG. Don't be upset. (*Looks about impatiently.*) You know, when you get on your feet I'll help you hang the new drapes.

SYLVIA. I started to . . .

GELLBURG. But they've been here over a month.

SYLVIA. Well this happened, I'm sorry.

GELLBURG. You have to occupy yourself is all I'm saying, Sylvia, you can't give in to this.

SYLVIA (*near an outbreak*). Well I'm sorry – I'm sorry about everything!

GELLBURG. Please, don't get upset, I take it back! (*A moment; stalemate.*)

SYLVIA. I wonder what my tests show. (GELLBURG *is silent.*) That the specialist did.

GELLBURG. I went to see Dr Hyman last night.

SYLVIA. You did? Why didn't you mention it?

GELLBURG. I wanted to think over what he said.

SYLVIA. What did he say?

(*With a certain deliberateness* GELLBURG *goes over to her and gives her a kiss on the cheek. She is embarrassed and vaguely alarmed.*)

SYLVIA. Phillip! (*A little uncomprehending laugh.*)

GELLBURG. I want to change some things. About the way I've been doing.

(*He stands there for a moment perfectly still, then rolls her chair closer to the upholstered chair in which he now sits and takes her hand. She doesn't quite know what to make of his, but doesn't remove her hand.*)

SYLVIA. Well what did he say?

GELLBURG (*he pats her hand*). I'll tell you in a minute. I'm thinking about a Dodge.

SYLVIA. A Dodge?

GELLBURG. I want to teach you to drive. So you can go where you like, visit your mother in the afternoon. – I want you to be happy, Sylvia.

SYLVIA (*surprised*). Oh.

GELLBURG. We have the money, we could do a lot of things. Maybe see Washington, DC. It's supposed to be a very strong car, you know.

SYLVIA. But aren't they all black? – Dodges?

GELLBURG. Not all. I've seen a couple of green ones.

SYLVIA. You like green?

GELLBURG. It's only a colour. You'll get used to it. – Or Chicago. It's really a big city, you know.

SYLVIA. Tell me what Dr Hyman said.

GELLBURG (*gets himself set*). He thinks it could all be coming from your mind. Like a . . . a fear of some kind got into you. Psychological. (SYLVIA *is still, listening*). Are you afraid of something?

SYLVIA (*a slow shrug, a shake of her head*). . . . I don't know, I don't think so. What kind of fear, what does he mean?

GELLBURG. Well, he explains it better, but . . . like in a

22

war, people get so afraid they go blind temporarily. What they call shell-shock. But once they feel safer it goes away.

SYLVIA (*thinks about this a moment*). What about the tests the Mount Sinai men did?

GELLBURG. They can't find anything wrong with your body.

SYLVIA. But I'm numb!

GELLBURG. He claims being very frightened could be doing it. – Are you?

SYLVIA. I don't know.

GELLBURG. Personally . . . can I tell you what I think?

SYLVIA. What.

GELLBURG. I think it's this whole Nazi business.

SYLVIA. But it's in the paper – they're smashing up the Jewish stores . . . should I not read the paper? The streets are covered with broken glass!

GELLBURG. Yes, but you don't have to be constantly . . .

SYLVIA. It's ridiculous. I can't move my legs from reading a newspaper?

GELLBURG. He didn't say that; but I'm wondering if you're too involved with . . .

SYLVIA. It's ridiculous.

GELLBURG. Well, you talk to him tomorrow. (*Pause. He comes back to her and takes her hand, his need open.*) You've got to get better, Sylvia.

SYLVIA (*she sees his tortured face and tries to laugh*). What is this, am I dying or something?

GELLBURG. How can you say that?

SYLVIA. I've never seen such a look in your face.

GELLBURG. Oh no-no-no . . . I'm just worried.

SYLVIA. I don't understand what's happening . . . (*She turns away on the verge of tears.*)

GELLBURG. . . . I never realized . . . (*Sudden sharpness.*) . . . look at me, will you? (*She turns to him; he glances down*

23

at the floor.) I wouldn't know what to do without you, Sylvia, honest to God. I . . . (*Immense difficulty*.) I love you.

SYLVIA (*a dead, bewildered laugh*). What is this?

GELLBURG. You have to get better. If I'm ever doing something wrong I'll change it. Let's try to be different. All right? And you too, you've got to do what the doctors tell you.

SYLVIA. What can I do? Here I sit and they say there's nothing wrong with me.

GELLBURG. Listen . . . I think Hyman is a very smart man . . . (*He lifts her hand and kisses her knuckle; embarrassed and smiling*.) When we were talking, something came to mind; that maybe if we could sit down with him, the three of us, and maybe talk about . . . you know . . . everything.

(*Pause*.)

SYLVIA. That doesn't matter any more, Phillip.

GELLBURG (*an embarrassed grin*). How do you know? Maybe . . .

SYLVIA. It's too late for that.

GELLBURG (*once launched he is terrified*). Why? Why is it too late?

SYLVIA. I'm surprised you're still worried about it.

GELLBURG. I'm not worried, I just think about it now and then.

SYLVIA. Well, it's too late, dear, it doesn't matter any more, it hasn't for years. (*She draws back her hand*.) (*Pause*.)

GELLBURG. . . . Well, all right. But if you wanted to I'd . . .

SYLVIA. We did talk about it, I took you to Rabbi Steiner about it twice, what good did it do?

GELLBURG. In those days I still thought it would change by itself. I was so young, I didn't understand such

24

things. It came out of nowhere and I thought it would go the same way.

SYLVIA. I'm sorry, Phillip, it didn't come out of nowhere.

(*Silent,* GELLBURG *evades her eyes.*)

SYLVIA. You regretted you got married.

GELLBURG. I didn't 'regret it' . . .

SYLVIA. You did, dear. You don't have to be ashamed of it.

(*A long silence.*)

GELLBURG. I'm going to tell you the truth – in those days I thought that if we separated I wouldn't die of it. I admit that.

SYLVIA. I always knew that.

GELLBURG. But I haven't felt that way in years now.

SYLVIA. Well, I'm here. (*Spreads her arms out, a wildly ironical look in her eyes.*) Here I am, Phillip!

GELLBURG (*offended*). The way you say that is not very . . .

SYLVIA. Not very what? I'm here; I've been here a long time.

GELLBURG (*a helpless surge of anger*). I'm trying to tell you something!

SYLVIA (*openly taunting him now*). But I said I'm here! (GELLBURG *moves about as she speaks, as though trying to find an escape or a way in.*) I'm here for my mother's sake, and Jerome's sake and everybody's sake except mine, but I'm here and here I am. And now finally you want to talk about it, now when I'm turning into an old woman? How do you want me to say it? Tell me, dear, I'll say it the way you want me to. What should I say?

GELLBURG (*insulted and guilty*). I want you to stand up.

SYLVIA. I can't stand up.

(GELLBURG *takes both her hands.*)

GELLBURG. You can. Now come on. Stand up.

SYLVIA. I can't!

GELLBURG. You can stand up, Sylvia. Now lean on me and get on your feet. (*He pulls her up; then steps aside releasing her; she collapses on the floor. He stands over her.*) What are you trying to do? (*He goes to his knees to yell into her face.*) What are you trying to do, Sylvia! (*She looks at him in terror at the mystery before her.*) (*Blackout.*)

COMMENTARY: This scene is full of contrast between the two characters as their personalities and motivations come into open conflict. Sylvia has just got rid of her sister and has turned again to her newspapers when she is unexpectedly disturbed by Phillip's awkward arrival. Think how unusual this must be for both of them – Phillip is the kind of man who would never leave work early let alone bearing a gift, even if it is only pickles. Throughout their marriage they have kept their genuine emotions and feelings about one another bottled up. There is no easy verbal or physical familiarity between them. The doctor has told Phillip to give Sylvia 'a lot of loving' and as we see in this scene affection doesn't come easily for him. Phillip 'adores' his wife but in an almost pathological way – he needs her for his very survival. He knows how to talk business and can strike a hard bargain, but here he is inept and uneasy trying to deal with emotional and personal problems. He is full of the best intentions to cure Sylvia, but on his own terms, offering Sylvia different 'deals' to distract her. She seems weary of Phillip and gives him only the most nominal of responses: 'that's nice', 'that's sad', etc. As the scene progresses, Sylvia's mood towards Phillip changes from apparent calm indifference to outright anger and sarcasm. Notice that while Phillip is desperate to get Sylvia to walk again right here and now, she is strangely unconcerned and resigned to her plight. Sylvia is a complacent and willing invalid with an apparently insistent capacity for suffering.

Closer
Patrick Marber

Act 1, scene 1. Hospital. Early morning. London. 1993.

Alice (early 20s) is 'a girl from the town'. She has been working in New York as a stripper and has recently returned to London. She is an independent free spirit but refers to herself as a 'waif'. In the school of hard knocks she has learned to be tough, aggressive and purposeful. She wants everything and expects nothing. Dan (30s) is 'a man from the suburbs'. He is a frustrated writer who works for one of the London papers writing obituaries. Dan is a cynical and watchful wise guy. His life has become somewhat aimless and he drifts along from day to day barely aware of what he wants or expects from life. This scene opens the play.

(ALICE *is sitting. She is wearing a black coat. She has a rucksack by her side. Also a brown leather briefcase. She rolls down one sock. She has a cut on her leg. Quite bloody. She looks at it. She picks some strands of wool from the wound.* ALICE *looks in her rucksack and finds a box of matches. She lights a match, watches it burn, blows it out. She looks at the briefcase. Thinks. Looks around. Opens it. She searches inside. She pulls out some sandwiches in silver foil and a green apple. She opens the sandwiches and looks at the contents, smiles, puts them back. She shines the apple. She bites into it. As she starts to chew* DAN *enters. He wears a suit and an overcoat. He stops, watches her eating his apple. He is holding two hot drinks in styrofoam cups.*)

ALICE. Sorry. I was looking for a cigarette.

DAN. I gave up.

ALICE. Well, try harder.

(DAN *hands her a drink.*)

ALICE. Have you got to be somewhere?

DAN. Work. Didn't fancy my sandwiches?

ALICE. I don't eat fish.

DAN. Why not?

ALICE. Fish piss in the sea.

DAN. So do children.

ALICE. I don't eat children either. What's your work?

DAN. Journalism.

ALICE. What sort?

DAN. Obituaries.

ALICE. Do you like it . . . in the dying business?

DAN. *Everyone's* in the dying business.

ALICE. Dead people aren't.

(*Beat.*)

Do you think a doctor will come?

DAN. Eventually. Does it hurt?

ALICE. I'll live.

DAN. Shall I put your leg up?

ALICE. Why?

DAN. That's what people do in these situations.

ALICE. What is this 'situation'?

(*Beat.*)

DAN. Do you want me to put your leg up?

ALICE. Yes, please.

(*He lifts her leg onto a chair.*)

Who cut off your crusts?

DAN. Me.

ALICE. Did your mother cut off your crusts when you were a little boy?

DAN. I believe she did, yes.

ALICE. You should eat your crusts.

DAN. You should stop smoking.

(*Beat.*)

I've got a mobile, is there anyone you'd like to phone?

ALICE. I don't know anyone.

(*Beat.*)

Thank you for scraping me off the road.

DAN. My pleasure.

ALICE. You knight.

(DAN *looks at her.*)

DAN. You damsel.

(*Beat.*)

Why didn't you look?

ALICE. I never look where I'm going.

DAN. I looked into your eyes and then you stepped into the road.

ALICE. Then what?

DAN. You were lying on the ground, you focused on me, you said, 'Hallo, stranger.'

ALICE. What a slut.

DAN. I noticed your leg was cut.

ALICE. Did you notice my legs?

DAN. In what sense?

ALICE. In the sense of 'nice legs'?

DAN. Quite possibly.

ALICE. Then what?

DAN. The cabbie got out. He crossed himself. He said, 'Thank fuck, I thought I'd killed her.' I said, 'Let's get her to a hospital.' He hesitated, I think he thought there'd be paperwork and he'd be held responsible. So I said, with a slight sneer, 'Please, just drop us at the hospital.'

ALICE. Show me the sneer.

(DAN *sneers.*)

ALICE. Very good.

DAN. We put you in the cab and came here.

ALICE. What was I doing?

29

DAN. You were murmuring, 'I'm very sorry for all the inconvenience.' I had my arm round you, your head was on my shoulder.

ALICE. Was my head . . . 'lolling'?

DAN. That's exactly what it was doing.

(*Pause.*)

ALICE. You have the saddest looking bun I've ever seen. Can I have it?

(DAN *opens his briefcase.*)

ALICE. You'll be late for work.

DAN. Are you saying you want me to go?

ALICE. No.

(*She puts her hand in the briefcase.*)

DAN. You can have half.

(*She removes the bun, tears it in two and begins to eat.*)

Why were you at Blackfriars Bridge?

ALICE. I'd been dancing at a club near Smithfield. I went for a walk. I went to see the meat being unloaded.

DAN. The carcasses?

ALICE. Yes.

DAN. Why?

ALICE. Because they're repulsive. Then I found a tiny park . . . it's a graveyard too. Postman's Park. Do you know it?

(DAN *shakes his head.*)

ALICE. There's a memorial to ordinary people who died saving the lives of others. It's most curious. Then I decided to go to Borough . . . so I went to Blackfriars Bridge to cross the river.

(*Pause.* DAN *offers her the other half of the bun.*)

ALICE. Are you sure?

DAN. Yeah, it's yesterday's sad bun.

(*Beat.*)

That park . . . it's near here?

(ALICE *nods.*)

DAN. Is there a statue?

ALICE. A Minotaur.

DAN. I do know it . . . we sat there . . . (my mother's dead) . . . my father and I sat there the afternoon she died. She died here actually . . . she was a smoker. My father . . . ate . . . an egg sandwich . . . I remember his hands shaking with grief . . . pieces of egg falling onto the grass . . . butter on his top lip . . . but I don't remember . . . a memorial. (*Pause.*)

ALICE. Is your father still alive?

DAN. Just. He's in a home.

ALICE. How did you end up writing obituaries? What did you really want to be?

(*Pause.*)

DAN. Oh . . . I had dreams of being a writer but I had no voice – no talent. So . . . I ended up in the 'Siberia' of journalism.

ALICE. Tell me what you do. I want to imagine you in . . . Siberia.

DAN. Really?

ALICE. Yes.

DAN. Well . . . we call it 'the obits page'. There's three of us; me, Harry and Graham. The first thing someone will say (usually Graham) is 'Who's on the slab?' Meaning did anyone important die overnight. Are you sure you want to know?

ALICE. Yes.

DAN. If someone did die we go to the 'deep freeze' which is a computer containing all the obituaries and we'll find the dead person's life.

ALICE. People's obituaries are already written when they're still alive?

DAN. Mmhmm. If no one important has died then Harry – he's the editor – decides who we lead with and we check facts, make calls, polish the prose. Some days I might be

31

asked to deal with the widows or widowers. They try to persuade us to run an obituary of their husbands or wives. They feel we're dishonouring their loved ones if we don't ... but ... most of them are ... well, there isn't the space. At six we stand round the computer and read the next day's page, make final changes, put in a few euphemisms to amuse ourselves ...

ALICE. Such as?

DAN. 'He was a clubbable fellow', meaning he was an alcoholic. 'He valued his privacy' – gay. 'He enjoyed his privacy' – raging queen. 'She was a convivial hostess' –

ALICE. A pissed old slapper?

DAN. Exactly.

(*Pause. ALICE strokes DAN's face. He is surprised but not unwilling.*)

ALICE. And what would your euphemism be ...

DAN. For me?

ALICE. Mmm.

DAN. He was ... 'reserved'.

ALICE. A lonely old bastard?

DAN. Perhaps.

ALICE. And me?

DAN. You were ... 'disarming'.

(*Beat.*)

ALICE. How did you get this job?

DAN. They ask you to write your own obituary ... and ... if it amuses, you're in.

(*They are close, looking at each other.*)

COMMENTARY: In this quintessential urban play Marber explores the twin imperatives of sexual jealousy and sexual desire. The accident which randomly throws Dan and Alice together acts as a catalyst for both of them to become 'closer'. Despite the potentially inauspicious beginning, there seems to be a mutual interest between them. Dan is aware that there was a frisson of attraction from the moment he made eye contact with Alice just before the accident. A wary curiosity informs their bantering exchange; they are testing and teasing each other. Alice is impulsive and confrontational and at times she sounds like a naive but articulate child, trying to provoke a reaction. She likes to think she is in control of her destiny and her sexuality, 'I know what men want . . . Men want a girl who looks like a boy. They want to protect her but she must be a survivor. And she must come . . . like a train . . . but with elegance.' Dan, although more circumspect and conventional, seems charmed by her flirtatious cheekiness and gamely goes along with Alice's baiting. Dan appears slightly goofy, impulsive and in need of mothering. Throughout the play Alice retains an enigmatic quality, no matter how 'close' she gets to people she never fully reveals herself. By the end of the play it turns out that even her name is a fiction.

Dog Opera
Constance Congdon

Act 1. Jones Beach on Long Island. New York. The present.

Madeline Newell (35 or so) is single and works as a librarian in a New York City elementary school. Peter Szczepanek (35 or so) is single, gay and works in an office. They have been best friends and confidants for the past twenty-five years; when they were both still at school Madeline had an abortion and Pete was there to hold her hand. They now see one another regularly and phone at least once a day. They are hip, urban and desperately seeking romance and relationships. In this scene they 'are semi-reclining in aluminum chaises on a public beach, under a beach umbrella. They are wearing T-shirts, hats, sunglasses and towels over their thighs. The are sharing a can of Diet Coke.'

PETE. There's just one thing . . .
MADELINE. What?
PETE. One thing I'm worried about.
MADELINE. What?
PETE. Will guys think I'm a transsexual?
MADELINE. You're too hairy.
PETE. I could be in transition.
MADELINE. If you'd take off that towel –
PETE. And let the world see my thighs?
I don't think so.
MADELINE. *Your* thighs? Puh-leeze.
PETE. There's nothing wrong with your thighs.
MADELINE. If Jacques Cousteau were here, I'd be on PBS. Okay?
(*Sees a guy.*) Oh man.

34

PETE. Where?

MADELINE. At three o'clock.

PETE. Now – wait a minute. Where is midnight?

MADELINE. Straight ahead.

PETE. And six is back here.

MADELINE. You're going to miss him.

PETE. Where?

MADELINE. I'm not pointing. Forget it.

PETE (*spying the guy*). Oh, wait a minute.
Blue Speedos?

MADELINE. Grey.

PETE. If you're quibbling about the color, how great can this guy be?

MADELINE. You missed him.

PETE (*sees another guy*). Whoa, doggies.

MADELINE. What is this? Jed Clampett cruises Jones Beach?

PETE. Lord have mercy.

MADELINE (*sees this guy*). Oh my.

PETE. Ohhhh. Ohhhhh. Mama.

MADELINE. A basket worthy of Carmen Miranda's head.

PETE. She'll have to fight me for him.

MADELINE. Buns.

PETE (*they take him in*). Buns.

MADELINE. Gay.

PETE. Straight.
(*Reconsidering.*) Straight.

MADELINE. Gay.

PETE. No way.

MADELINE. Invite him over.
If I fall in love with him – he's gay.

PETE. If I fall in love with him – he's straight.
(*Weakly.*) Oh, sir? Sir? Can you come over here and ruin our lives?

MADELINE. Oh, please, it's been at least two weeks.

PETE. Oh my God.

MADELINE. What?

PETE. He's looking at us.

MADELINE. Oh jeez.

PETE. I'm going to take off my towel.

MADELINE. That should do it.

PETE. What's that supposed to mean?

MADELINE. Peter, take off the towel.

(PETE *takes his towel off – he's wearing a long pair of black bathing trunks.*)

MADELINE. Those *are* fetching.

PETE. He's coming over, Madeline!

Oh fuck.

MADELINE. Will you relax?

PETE. He's looking at me.

MADELINE. I knew he was gay. He's motioning . . .

PETE. I've attracted a deaf-mute.

It'll be like *Children of a Lesser God.*

Oh my God! I'm Bill Hurt! (*To guy.*) What?

Oh no, I don't have any – sorry! I quit six months ago. (PETE *watches guy exit.*) But I'd be glad to make you one if you bring me the tobacco! (*Guy is gone.*) Or just bring me your seeds and we'll grow it together.

Or if you have a gun, I'd be glad to shoot myself in the other foot. (PETE *sits down.*) I'm sure he appreciated the lecture on quitting smoking.

MADELINE. It wasn't a lecture.

It was a comment.

PETE. He was gay, Madeline.

And he almost talked to me until I turned into Bobby Bizarro.

MADELINE. Pete – he was straight.

PETE. How do you know?

MADELINE. If he were gay, he would have talked to me, too.

PETE. You're right.

I wasn't just rejected.

MADELINE. You weren't just rejected.

PETE. I was asked for a cigarette.

And I didn't have any.

MADELINE. That simple. (*Long beat.*) I was rejected.

He didn't even talk to me.

I don't know – maybe the towel makes me look fatter.

PETE. Take it off.

MADELINE. When pigs fly. (*Beat.*) When pigs fly, maybe I'll join the air force – at last, a suit that fits me.

PETE. Stop it.

I like that black thing you bought.

MADELINE. Which black thing? All my clothes are black.

PETE. The dressy suit thing.

MADELINE. Oh, my memorial outfit?

PETE. I guess so.

MADELINE. It's ten years old!

I bought it for . . . Barry.

PETE. Barry.

Barry's memorial.

That's an old suit.

MADELINE. Too old.

Burn it.

Take it out and burn it.

I need a new suit, Peter.

PETE. Me, too.

Hey! Hey, hey, hey!

What are we doin'?

MADELINE. We are cruisin'.

We are strategically placed just to the left of Field Six at Jones Beach, so the pickin's are great.

PETE. And the livin' is easy.

MADELINE. Straight men to the left of me.

PETE. Gay men to the right of me.

MADELINE. Into the valley of . . . *life*
Rode the six hundred.

PETE. And that's why there are no cute guys –
Six hundred hunky light brigade officers rode up –

MADELINE. And took the cute ones – (*Sees a guy.*)
– wait a minute. Nine o'clock. Approaching –

PETE. Now, where's nine again?

MADELINE (*showing him quickly*). Noon. Three. Six.
Nine.

PETE (*sees him*). Very attractive black man?

MADELINE. Red Speedos.

PETE. Oh my God.
Remind me to make an offering to the god of nylon.

MADELINE. All synthetic fibers aren't bad. (*They watch him.*)

PETE. Well, that made my afternoon.

MADELINE. Yeah. (*Still watching as he disappears down the beach.*)

PETE. Gay? Straight?

MADELINE. Beautiful.

COMMENTARY: *Dog Opera* humorously examines the emotionally intimate friendship between a gay man and a straight woman. This scene requires careful playing to achieve a balance between the flip comedy and the characters' genuine anxiety. Madeline and Pete are 'cruisin' the beach without moving a muscle. It is vital to create the world of the beach for your audience; the warm sun, the relaxed indolence, the sense of the other people and especially the 'cute guys'. The clock device should help you to animate and people the beach. Madeline and Pete's voyeurism gives the scene its unique comic flavour. The two friends have an easy familiarity and a camaraderie which is never threatened by rivalry. Notice how they both suffer from lack of confidence and indulge in bouts of comic self-deprecation. They are passing the time, assessing the action and desperately trying to judge the sexuality of all the 'beautiful' men.

The Heidi Chronicles
Wendy Wasserstein

Act 1, scene 1. A high-school gym in Chicago, with folding chairs, streamers and a table with a punch bowl. 1965.

Heidi Holland (16) is wearing a traditional A-line dress. She is a hard-working student at the elite Miss Crain's school where she edits the school newspaper. She has come to this high-school dance with her best friend, Susan, who is eager to find a dance partner, whereas Heidi prefers sitting and watching on the sidelines. When she is approached by a boy she gives him a sardonic cold shoulder. Peter (16) is wearing a St Mark's school blazer. He is also a highly motivated, articulate and academic student. As the scene begins Susan has just left Heidi who 'sits on a chair, takes out a book, reads it for a moment, then puts it on her lap as she stares out. "Play with fire" is played. Peter . . . approaches. She smiles and looks down.'

PETER. You must be very bright.
HEIDI. Excuse me?
PETER. You look so bored you must be very bright.
HEIDI. I'm sorry?
PETER. Don't be sorry. I appreciate bored people. Bored, depressed, anxious. These are the qualities I look for in a woman. Your lady friend is dancing with the gentleman who looks like Bobby Kennedy. I find men who smoke and twist at the same time so dreary.
HEIDI. Not worth the coordination, really.
PETER. Do you have any?
HEIDI. I can sit and read at the same time.
PETER. What book is that?
HEIDI. *Death Be Not Proud.*

PETER. Of course.

HEIDI. A favorite of mine at dances.

PETER. I was drawn to you from the moment I saw you shielding that unfortunate wench rolling up her garments in the tempest.

HEIDI. I'm sorry.

PETER. Please. Don't apologize for being the most attractive woman on this cruise.

HEIDI. Cruise?

PETER. She docks tonight in Portsmouth. And then farewell to the *Queen Mary*. Forever to harbor in Long Beach, California. *C'est triste, n'est pas?*

HEIDI. *Ce n'est pas bon.*

PETER (*excitedly*). Our tragic paths were meant to cross. I leave tomorrow for the sanatorium in Zurich. (*Coughs.*)

HEIDI. How odd! I'm going to the sanatorium in Milan. (*Coughs. He offers her his handkerchief. She refuses.*)

PETER. My parents are heartbroken. They thought I was entering Williams College in the fall.

HEIDI. My parents put down a deposit at Vassar.

PETER. We've only this night together. I'm Peter, a small noise from Winnetka. I tried to pick out your name . . . Amanda, Lady Clara, Estelle . . .

HEIDI. It's . . .

PETER. No, don't tell me. I want to remember you as you are. Beside me in the moonlight, the stars above us . . .

HEIDI. The sea below us.

PETER. Glenn Miller and the orchestra. It's all so peaceful.

HEIDI. Mmmmmm. Quite peaceful.

(*'The Shoop Shoop Song' is heard again.*)

PETER. The twist-and-smokers are heaving themselves on their lady friends. This must be the final song. Would you do me the honor of one dance?

HEIDI. Certainly.

PETER. Ahhh! 'The Shoop Shoop Song'. Baroque but fragile.

HEIDI. Melodic but atonal.

PETER. Will you marry me?

HEIDI. I covet my independence.

PETER. Perhaps when you leave the sanatorium, you'll think otherwise. I want to know you all my life. If we can't marry, let's be great friends.

HEIDI. I will keep your punch cup, as a memento, beside my pillow.

PETER. Well, shall we hully-gully, baby?

HEIDI. Really, I . . .

PETER. Don't worry, I'll teach you.

(*He begins to do a form of shimmy line dance. Holding* HEIDI*'s hand, he instructs her. The dance is somewhat interpretive and becomes a minuet. They sing as they dance together.*)

PETER.

How 'bout the way he acts?

HEIDI.

Oh, noooo, that's not the way.

PETER.

And you're not listenin' to all I say.

If you wanna know if he loves you so . . .

(*Takes* HEIDI'S *waist and dips her.*)

PETER.

It's in his kiss.

HEIDI & PETER.

Oh, yeah! It's in his kiss!

(*They continue to dance as the lights fade.*)

COMMENTARY: This play follows the progress of American baby-boomer Heidi Holland from high school to early middle age. Heidi really doesn't want to be at this party with its old-fashioned courtship rituals. She obviously planned on being a party pooper since she brought a book along with her. She has an extremely ironic sensibility which gets in the way of her enjoying the party to the full. That is until Peter comes along whose own sardonic and theatrical attitudes seem to be perfectly in tune with Heidi's. His charm and ironic wit quickly break down her reserve and together they create a hammy parody of B-movie romantic dialogue. They are both slightly unusual, eccentric and, as it turns out, soulmates. They remain friends but never become lovers. The play reveals that fifteen years later Peter, much to Heidi's surprise and disappointment, is a 'liberal-homosexual pediatrician'.

The Lodger
Simon Burke

Scene 1. A bed-sitting room in Wise's house. A small, dreary suburban town somewhere north of King's Cross.

Andrew Wise (mid 40s) has 'a calm exterior – phlegmatic with a slow burn. He is still attractive, in a rugged and physical sort of way, but obviously has no interest in fashion.' Lois ('lost somewhere in her thirties but perhaps looks older') is 'a beautiful woman who has, perhaps, had more than her share of troubles. She is dressed smartly, but not fashionably, for business.' The play begins with this scene. Wise 'is shy and ill at ease as he turns to hold the door open' for Lois.

WISE. This is the room. Obviously.
(*His accent is Southern working-middle class. LOIS looks round. It is a poor little room, unloved and unlit. The fixtures and fittings are as cheap as may be procured anywhere and there are as few of them as possible.*)
LOIS. And thirty quid a week, yeah?
WISE. Er, yes. If er . . . if that's all right . . .
(*She casts a dubious eye over the fittings.*)
LOIS. Well, it seems a pretty shit deal for living here but, what the hell, I need the money.
(*He stares at her blankly. She smiles, which softens her careworn features.*)
It was a joke.
(*WISE nods seriously as she moves over to test the bed for squeaks. She sits down on it and pulls out a pack of cigarettes. Her accent betrays an education and a professional upbringing.*)

LOIS. Do you smoke?

WISE. No.

LOIS. Do you mind if I have one?

(*She doesn't wait for an answer.* WISE *does mind, but says nothing about it.*)

WISE. You're not from round here then?

LOIS. No.

WISE. From London?

LOIS. Yeah.

WISE. You working up here?

LOIS. For a bit.

WISE. So you wouldn't be here long?

LOIS. Hard to say. Does the thirty quid include the questions?

WISE. Well, obviously, if you're going to be living here, I want to know a bit about you.

LOIS. I want a room, not a relationship.

WISE. It's not that –

LOIS. I like my privacy.

(*He backs off, chastened.*)

WISE. Sorry – I haven't done this before.

LOIS. I have. It's easy: I give you money. You give me key.

WISE. Right. Yes.

LOIS. Who else lives here then?

WISE. Just me at the moment.

LOIS. So you're not married?

WISE. No.

LOIS. You've got a wedding ring.

(WISE *looks at his ring finger, then puts his hands in his pockets.*)

How come you're renting the room out?

WISE. Well, the money'll be useful. Obviously.

LOIS. You don't work then? As such.

WISE. Yes, no, I do, but the mortgage and everything . . .

45

I bought at the top of the market. It's hard to sell . . .
Things have become a bit tight recently . . . you know . . .
(*She nods sympathetically as he trails off. She sits on the bed,
apparently relaxed and self-possessed, but the way she smokes
hungrily gives a hint at something more brittle beneath the
surface, even desperate. She has a distinct but understated
sexual allure. She is aware of her body and knows how to use it.
She is not using it on* WISE.)

LOIS. So, what do you do then?

WISE. Oh I work in security . . . Shift work . . . It varies.
And you?

LOIS. What's it matter what I do? I want a room, not a
job.

(*She looks at him blankly, puzzled. He's flustered, on the back
foot.*)

WISE. Well, I'm asking what you do, just, because, to be
sure you can afford the rent. That's all . . .

LOIS. If I couldn't afford the rent, why would I come
here? I mean, you'd ask me for the rent, and I wouldn't
have it and you'd throw me out and I'd have nowhere to
live. Why would I do that?

(WISE *has to laugh, though not with much humour. She
relents*:)

All right. I'm a researcher. For a market research company.

WISE. Sounds interesting.

LOIS. It's a job. It's not *supposed* to be interesting. I work
when I like, choose my own times. It's OK.

WISE. I'm surprised they don't put you up in a hotel . . .
(*She considers him coolly.*)

LOIS. OK, I'll be honest: they give me an allowance for a
hotel, but if I can get cheaper accommodation, I can keep
the change, right? We're not supposed to, but no one
minds.

WISE. Researching what?

46

(*The faintest flicker of hesitation, which she covers by blowing a smoke ring.* WISE *opens a window.*)

LOIS. Social trends. I'm sorry, I'm not supposed to tell people the details. Bit pathetic, but there you are. It's a government contract. There. Feel better now?

WISE. No offence.

LOIS. Are you saying, you don't want anything to do with people on the dole, is what you're hinting?

WISE. No, not particularly –

LOIS. A lot of landlords don't want unemployed people.

WISE. No . . . Obviously.

LOIS. In case their rent payments go on record.

(*He frowns, then gets her meaning.*)

WISE. There's nothing below board about this.

LOIS. But you'd prefer cash?

(*He looks at her uncertainly. She smiles.*)

Don't worry, I'm not from the Inland Revenue.

WISE. I'm not worried. This is all perfectly kosher.

LOIS. Sure, sure, I just like to know who I'm dealing with, that's all, nothing personal – just business.

WISE. Obviously. Business.

LOIS. OK. I'll take it. I'll give you cash in advance, two weeks' if you want.

(*She rummages through her shoulder bag.*)

WISE. Oh, fine. OK. Ah, do you have references?

LOIS. References?

(*She looks up at him, half amused, half irritated.*)

WISE. Yes . . . Bank, or employer . . . Or something . . .

LOIS. I'm sorry, I've forgotten your name –

WISE. Wise. Andrew Wise.

LOIS. OK, Andrew, are you going to give *me* references? Are you going to give me, for example, letters from two people who've lived here?

WISE. What?

LOIS. I mean, if anyone needs references, it's me that

needs references not you, especially as I'm a girl. I mean I don't know *anything* about you. I don't even know this is actually your house. Do I? You could be any one.

WISE. This is silly.

LOIS. Is it? I suppose women don't get raped any more. What a *relief*.

WISE. No, obviously, I'm sorry, I didn't mean that . . .

LOIS. OK, Andrew, what are you worried about? I mean, am I likely to ruin your career? Destroy your life as you know it? You think that's likely? Kill you maybe?

WISE. No, no. It's just that it's *normal*, you know, references. It's what tenants give landlords.

LOIS. Come on I mean you own this room, you own this house, so you say, you can decide whether to let me live here or not on the vaguest whim, you can beat me up and throw me out at a second's notice and me I have to have a strange man sleeping next door after what I've been through it seems to me I'm the one that needs protection, fucking references is what it seems I need. Me . . .

WISE. I'm sorry. I didn't mean to upset you.

LOIS. That's OK. You didn't . . . It's just a question of trust.

WISE. Look, I'm sorry . . . it's just (*Groping for an excuse.*) there's someone else coming to look at the room.

(*She looks round at him.*)

LOIS. Is there? You just made that up, didn't you?

WISE (*flustered*). No, no . . . I didn't.

LOIS. OK, who's coming then?

(WISE *hesitates. She runs her hands through her hair; she suddenly looks exhausted.*)

It's *such* a bad lie. I've come a long way and I'm shattered and I think I deserve a much better one.

WISE. Look –

LOIS. Excuse me, wait a minute. I can't believe my ears – are you saying, is someone actually saying, I'm not good

48

enough to live here? *Here*? What sort of person isn't good enough to live *here*?

WISE. Thanks for coming. I hope you find somewhere you like. Suitable.

(*She realises he is serious and stares at him, stunned.*)

LOIS. Look, Andrew, I mean, look at this place. Look at it. Who're you expecting to rent this? I mean, *what*? You think maybe Japanese businessmen looking for a pied-à-terre maybe, or maybe like Fergie and her mates looking for a little hideaway, I mean what sort of person you expect here? I mean, I have clothes. I *wash*. Which seems to me more than you can reasonably expect for this room, is what seems to me. I even have money. Cash.

(WISE *clearly hates a row.*)

I've never heard such a fuss about a thirty-quid room before.

WISE. Well, it's just, I live here too. It's not just business. Exactly.

(*Her temper subsides . . . She takes a deep breath.*)

LOIS. Sure, OK. I'm sorry. Look, I'm tired and wet and bad-tempered and I've nowhere else to go and it's late and it's raining. This is OK and I want to stay. Here, take the money.

(*She holds it towards him, but he doesn't take it.*)

WISE. I'm sorry. I don't think this is going to work out.

LOIS. You're thinking, maybe you and me, we've maybe got off on the wrong foot, is what you're thinking yeah?

WISE (*incredulous*). Well, maybe.

LOIS. It's OK, I don't hold grudges. (*She smiles.*) And I won't need a deposit.

(*He returns her smile nervously.*)

WISE. Look, Miss –

LOIS. Lois.

WISE. I'm sorry . . .

(*He sighs. A moment. Her face crumples. She starts to weep. He simply can't cope with this.*)

LOIS. Where do you want me to go?

WISE. I don't know . . . Where did you come from?

LOIS. A shitty bed and breakfast by the station. It was horrible.

WISE. I'm sorry . . . look . . . Lois . . . Please . . .

LOIS. You want me to go back *there*?

WISE. No, no – look . . . it's just . . .

(*He trails off miserably. She looks up at him hopefully with tearful, mascara-smudged eyes.*)

LOIS (*sniff*). Or do you want me to go to the Inland Revenue?

WISE. What?

(*She dries her eyes miserably. A moment. He can't believe his ears. She smiles tearfully up at him.*)

LOIS. Please can't I stay?

(*His mouth hangs open a second.*)

WISE. I've got nothing to hide.

LOIS. No, of course. It's just a question of trust.

(*She puts the money on the bedside table. He looks at it, then her, unable to talk. Then the phone rings. As if in a dream, he goes to answer it.*)

WISE. Hello . . . No, er . . . the room . . . yes . . .

(*The moment hangs and grows with his physical discomfort.*)

No . . . I'm afraid it's just been taken. Thank you.

(*He puts the phone down.*)

(*Blackout.*)

COMMENTARY: This play portrays the angst of lonely people driven to desperation. All the characters conceal their motives and intentions. Wise claims to be a security guard; Lois claims to be in market research. Both, of course, are lying and although the actors must be aware of this they should be very careful how they use this knowledge. It must inform the evasive way the characters behave; both of them are hiding their true identities for a reason. She is tired and bolshy; he is shy and uncertain of what he is doing. They have both been injured emotionally and physically in the past and they are extremely wary and suspicious of new people. They ruthlessly interrogate each other with limited success. Notice how each question is met with a deflected evasion. The more he probes the more suspicious she in turn becomes. Wise is really a Detective Constable in the CID. He is lonely and desperate since his wife left him and has resorted, unsuccessfully, to a computer dating agency. Lois is a prostitute with a drug habit who has fled London and her violent pimp. She has come to Wise's house as a temporary refuge. How desperate is she? Why does Wise, after so much resistance, finally give in?

The Pitchfork Disney
Philip Ridley

'Night. A dimly lit room in the East End of London: front door with many bolts . . . Everything old and colourless.'

Presley and Haley Stray are twenty-eight-year-old twins. 'Presley is dressed in dirty pyjamas, vest, frayed cardigan and slippers. He is unshaven, hair unevenly hacked very short, teeth discoloured, skin pale, dark rings beneath bloodshot eyes.' Haley 'is wearing an old nightdress beneath a man's frayed dressing gown. Her hair is longer, but still unevenly cut. Teeth and complexion the same as Presley's.' The twins have lived together all their lives. They are both chocoholics; their addiction is so extreme that they survive solely on a diet of chocolate. When they were eighteen years old their parents mysteriously 'disappeared', and since then their relationship has become increasingly obsessive; they are both still virgins. The only bequest from their parents was a supply of medicine and tranquilisers that they ration between themselves. Always in a state of terror and dread, they experience the world as a living nightmare. Macabre and bizarre fantasy defines their existence. Although they are in their late twenties they regress and behave like children: it is as if the clock stopped for them when they were ten years old. They live hermetically together in a fortified home, shunning all contact with the outside. Presley dominates their relationship, intimidating Haley by rationing their parents' leftover drugs to keep her docile. Presley is the historian of the uniquely bizarre version of their happy, golden childhood. Haley relies on Presley to recount key episodes for her. As the play opens, Haley 'is sitting at the table. She is fiddling with a tiny piece of chocolate wrapping paper.' Presley 'is staring into the darkness outside'.

(*Sounds of dogs howling outside.* HALEY *flinches, looks at* PRESLEY *anxiously.* PRESLEY *looks at her. The dogs*

continue howling. Pause. Sound of dogs fades. PRESLEY
looks out of the window. HALEY *continues to look anxious.*)

HALEY. Describe it.

PRESLEY. Again?

HALEY. Just once more, Presley.

PRESLEY (*sighing*). You said that last time.

HALEY. Did I? I don't remember.

PRESLEY. You know your trouble, Haley? You break
your promises. You say one thing but you mean another.
You don't play fair. Sometimes I think you're nothing but
a . . .

HALEY (*interrupting*). What?

PRESLEY. Oh, nothing.

HALEY. Go on. Say it.

PRESLEY. Well, a cheat.

HALEY. Don't call me that. It's not fair. Not after what
happened this morning.

PRESLEY. What do you mean?

HALEY. With the shopping, I mean.

PRESLEY. What about it?

HALEY. The chocolate, Presley. I'm talking about the
chocolate. You bought fruit and nut.

PRESLEY. So?

HALEY. You know I don't like fruit and nut. You know
it makes me sick. The nut gets caught between my teeth
and the raisins taste like bits of skin.

PRESLEY. How do you know what skin tastes like?

HALEY. I can use my imagination.

PRESLEY. Well, you used to like fruit and nut.

HALEY. I've never liked fruit and nut. *You* like fruit and
nut. You know my favourite is orange chocolate . . .

PRESLEY (*interrupting*). I didn't just buy fruit and nut. I
bought other things as well.

HALEY. What other things?

PRESLEY. Lots of things.

HALEY. You didn't tell me.

PRESLEY (*sighing*). I did, Haley.

HALEY. Well, I must have forgotten. Where are they?

PRESLEY. In the drawer.

(HALEY *goes to drawer in sideboard. She opens it, discovers many bars of different chocolate. The chocolate is in bright wrapping paper.*)

HALEY. Oh, Presley . . . I can see orange chocolate.

(*She takes chocolate bars to the table. Spreads them over the surface as if they're jewels.*)

HALEY. Come and eat, Presley.

PRESLEY. Don't want to.

HALEY. You're sulking now.

PRESLEY. You shouldn't accuse me of just buying fruit and nut.

HALEY. I'm sorry. It's just that I saw you eating a bar earlier. I assumed that's all there was. I can see now . . . there's a big selection . . . Come on. (*Picks up a bar of fruit and nut and waves it temptingly in the air.*) Fruit and nut. Fruit and nut.

(PRESLEY *and* HALEY *sit at the table and begin to eat chocolate.*)

PRESLEY. There's more chocolate than ever in the shops now, Haley. You go in and it sparkles like treasure. Flaky chocolate, mint chocolate, crispy chocolate . . .

HALEY (*overlapping*). . . . Bubbly chocolate . . .

PRESLEY (*overlapping*). . . . Wafer chocolate . . .

HALEY (*overlapping*). . . . Chocolate with cream in . . .

PRESLEY (*overlapping*). . . . Chocolate with nuts in . . .

HALEY (*overlapping*). . . . Which I don't like.

PRESLEY (*overlapping*). . . . Which you don't like. All sorts of chocolate in all sorts of paper.

(HALEY *is sorting through the pile for another bar of orange chocolate.*)

PRESLEY. . . . There's coffee chocolate and mint chocolate and strawberry chocolate and . . .

HALEY (*giving up her search*). Well, that's typical.

PRESLEY. What?

HALEY. You bought . . . (*Sorting through the pile of chocolate and counting.*) . . . one, two, three, four, plus the one you're eating, plus the one this morning, that's six bars of fruit and nut and only one bar of orange.

PRESLEY (*staring, chocolate in mouth*). I'm sorry. I must have got carried away.

HALEY. You did it on purpose.

PRESLEY. There's other things, Haley. Look! Flaky chocolate and bubbly chocolate and crispy rice chocolate . . .

HALEY (*firmly*). My favourite is orange chocolate. (*Pause.*) This is just like you, Presley. Sometimes you're so . . .

PRESLEY (*interrupting*). What?

HALEY. Oh, nothing.

PRESLEY. Go on. Say it.

HALEY. Well, selfish.

PRESLEY. Don't call me that. It's not fair. Not after what *you* did this morning.

HALEY. What did I do?

PRESLEY. About going out to get the shopping in the first place.

HALEY. What about it?

PRESLEY. You know it was your turn.

HALEY. Was not.

PRESLEY. Was!

HALEY. Wasn't!

PRESLEY. Was!

HALEY. Wasn't!

PRESLEY. Was! Was! Was!

HALEY. How? How was it my turn?

PRESLEY. Because I went yesterday. That's how.

HALEY. No you didn't.

PRESLEY. Yes I did. You know I did. I bought the milk and the bread. They were in a brown paper bag. I put them on the table. You were sitting where you're sitting now. You said, 'Didn't you buy any biscuits?' And I said, 'Yes.' I gave them to you. They were in a blue packet. I made you a cup of tea and you dunked the biscuits in the tea. Afterwards, I put the milk and what was left of the biscuits in the fridge.

HALEY. Biscuits? In the fridge?

PRESLEY. That's right.

HALEY. In a blue packet?

PRESLEY. Yes.

HALEY. A blue packet with yellow and red stripes?

PRESLEY. Yes.

HALEY. That means they're orange chocolate biscuits, Presley.

PRESLEY. I know.

HALEY. Well, why didn't you tell me? I've felt like a biscuit all day.

PRESLEY. But you saw me put them in the fridge.

HALEY. I forgot. You know I need reminding. If you make me a cup of tea and don't offer me a biscuit, then I assume all the biscuits have gone. I don't think you're hiding them from me.

PRESLEY. I wasn't hiding them . . .

HALEY (*standing*). Yes you were! You were going to wait for me to take my tablet, then eat them all yourself. (*Starts to make her way to the fridge.*)

PRESLEY. But I don't even like the biscuits. I got them for you. You're just trying to change the subject.

HALEY (*stopping in her tracks*). From what?

PRESLEY. From why you said it wasn't your turn to get the shopping when you know full well it was.

56

HALEY (*returning to the table*). Don't blame me. You remember what happened last time I went to the shops. It was terrible. I was so scared. I came back crying and shaking. My clothes were torn and wet. There was blood on my legs. You wiped it away with a tissue. I was crying so much I couldn't breathe properly. You remember that, Presley? I was hysterical. Wasn't I? Hysterical?

PRESLEY (*softly*). I suppose so.

HALEY. You were so nice. You put your arms round me and let me suck the dummy. You remember that?

PRESLEY. Yes.

COMMENTARY: Haley and Presley are like children in a fairy tale: innocents threatened by an evil (in this case nuclear) world. The siblings act like half-crazed, abandoned children. Living in such claustrophobic squalor they petulantly manipulate and menace each other. The minutiae of daily life become cause for constant conflict. Notice how childlike their language and behaviour are: they squabble, sulk and whine like jealous toddlers on the verge of terrible tantrums. Yet being adults they have the stamina to keep their squabbles going and growing. They live in utter fear of the unknown and the world outside. A trip to the shops is a perilous journey into the wild. The childhood trauma they appear to have suffered is never made entirely clear. Their only refuge is with each other. Notice how important visual things are to both twins; they relish the colours, textures and vividness of everything around them. Even mundane chocolate bars become technicolour jewels in their 'colourless' world. Their fixation with chocolate has mutated into an all-consuming sensual fetish. However, it is a challenge for the actors to convince the audience that the twins are real and not merely comic players in a surreal nightmare.

Raised in Captivity
Nicky Silver

Act 1, scene 3. The Dixons' living room. It is the middle of the night.

Bernadette (early 30s) and Kip Dixon (mid 30s) have been married for eight years. Kip is a dentist but hates teeth. He comes from a very poor background. After graduating from high school he robbed a man on the subway and used his credit cards to buy tickets to fly to Europe. He panhandled until he got a job as a guide at the 'depressing' Anne Frank House in Amsterdam. This was where he first met Bernadette who was on a European tour with her domineering mother. Bernadette is highly strung and often on the verge of tears: her twin brother, Sebastian, thinks she is 'completely insane'. As she is all too aware, her life has an aimless quality. She spends her time shopping, while her contemporaries pursue high-flying careers. She is obsessed with her weight and has a 'neurotic relationship with food'. Bernadette's mother recently died in a freak accident and this scene occurs the night after the funeral. 'Kip is looking out the window. After a moment Bernadette enters wearing a bathrobe.'

BERNADETTE. Kip?

KIP. Did I wake you?

BERNADETTE. What are you doing?

KIP. It's a beautiful night. The clouds have passed.

BERNADETTE. I woke up and the bed was empty. I didn't know where you were.

KIP. I didn't mean to wake you.

BERNADETTE. I got scared.

KIP. Come look at this.

BERNADETTE. Is something out there?

KIP. Come here.

BERNADETTE. I'm tired. It's been a very long, trying day.

KIP (*turning away*). Then go to bed.

BERNADETTE. Are you coming?

KIP. No.

BERNADETTE. What are you looking at? (*She goes to the window.*)

KIP. The moon.

BERNADETTE. The moon? The moon, Kip? You're looking at the moon?

KIP. Isn't it beautiful?

BERNADETTE. It looks dirty.

KIP. What would you call that color?

BERNADETTE (*exasperated*). White?

KIP. No, I don't think so. It's definitely not white.

BERNADETTE. Who cares?

KIP. Ecru, maybe. Or eggshell!

BERNADETTE. It's a big, dirty circle in the sky. Come back to bed.

KIP. Something happened today!

BERNADETTE. It's not that I'm not fascinated –

KIP. Listen to me.

BERNADETTE. Although, I'm not.

KIP. Do you realize that I never knew anyone who died before? It's true. My whole life, I never knew anyone who died. Isn't that startling?

BERNADETTE. I don't understand!

KIP. Did you know you're going to die? I didn't! I mean I had the information, tucked away in some remote corner of my brain, but seeing your mother, lifeless, still – seeing someone I didn't even like as an object made my own death a very tangible entity.

59

BERNADETTE. Everyone's going to die! Everyone who's born will die.

KIP. That's a very bleak point of view, Bernadette.

BERNADETTE. Life is finite. Thank God.

KIP (*with great importance*). I don't want to be a dentist.

BERNADETTE (*stunned, then*). No one *wants* to be a dentist!

KIP. I don't even know why I became one.

BERNADETTE. For the same reason as everyone else! You didn't have the grades for medical school.

KIP. Do you know what teeth are?

BERNADETTE. That's a rhetorical question, I assume.

KIP. They're millstones around my neck.

BERNADETTE. They are?

KIP. Yes.

BERNADETTE. Teeth?

KIP. They're dragging me down, into a vat of dire ugliness.

BERNADETTE. Teeth?

KIP. I look into mouths all day, and if I felt anything I'd burst into tears. I never mentioned it because I try to be positive.

BERNADETTE. Try harder.

KIP. I spend my life staring into gaping, gagging crypts filled with blood and drool.

BERNADETTE. That's very descriptive.

KIP (*excited*). I used to think I could make the mouth my canvas. I thought I could create the universe in miniature. But there is no poetry in teeth. When I was a child I saw things! I went to the museum with my mother. She dragged me from room to room, whispering into my ear the stories of the saints in the paintings. When I could, I ran off and found a room with a bench in the middle. I curled up and fell asleep. Then I opened my eyes. I saw a painting: *The City Rises* by Boccioni. It was beautiful, a scene of chaos with fire and horses and people in panic made up of a million splatters of color. And I stared at it. I studied it. And the colors came alive! Do you understand?

BERNADETTE. You had a dream.

KIP. I didn't! I don't know what it was, but it wasn't a dream! I told my father about it, that night at dinner. He broke all my crayons and lined the garbage with my drawing paper. He thought God was dead and I was proof.

BERNADETTE. I've lost the thread.

KIP. He taught me *not to see*.

BERNADETTE. What's the point of this!?

KIP (*after a moment, simply*). Do you love me, Bernadette?

BERNADETTE. Yes.

KIP. We're partners, aren't we?

BERNADETTE. Yes. Can we please go to bed?

KIP (*grandiose*). I'm going to be a painter! I want to learn to see again. I think it's possible.

BERNADETTE. That's what this is all about?

KIP. Don't belittle my rebirth!

BERNADETTE. Fine. Paint if you want. Paint until your arms fall off.

KIP. I mean full-time.

BERNADETTE. Pardon me?

KIP. I've looked into my last mouth.

BERNADETTE. You can't be serious!

KIP. You said you loved me. We're partners.

BERNADETTE (*in disbelief*). You're not going to work?

KIP. I'm going to work. I'm going to paint!

BERNADETTE. What kind of work is that?

KIP. Work worth doing. We don't need the money. We have your mother's now, and –

BERNADETTE. Oh my God ... Oh God. You're just –

61

KIP. Think of possibilities, Bernadette. You have no imagination.

BERNADETTE. I'm going to cry.

KIP. Do you want to go on like this for the rest of our lives?

BERNADETTE. Yes!

KIP. I want something else. You won't get what you don't want. I want a different kind of life.

BERNADETTE. I DON'T! There's nothing wrong with my life the way it is! I'm going to bed! I'd like to pretend this never happened. We never had this conversation.

KIP. Don't be angry. This is wonderful!

BERNADETTE. I think it's pretty goddamn terrible! I woke up this morning next to my husband, now – who are you?!

KIP. I'm me.

BERNADETTE. You are not! I don't want to talk about it.

KIP. I hoped you'd understand.

BERNADETTE. We'll talk about it in the morning.

KIP. I hoped you'd be happy.

BERNADETTE. I'm going to bed.

(KIP *takes her hand.*)

KIP. Look at me.

BERNADETTE (*angry*). What?

KIP. Everything looks new to me.

BERNADETTE. I'm tired.

(*He touches her face.*)

KIP. I've never seen you at all.

(*He takes her hand. She turns to leave. He doesn't release her.*)

BERNADETTE. Let go of me.

KIP. Your eyes.

BERNADETTE. It's late.

KIP. It's morning.

BERNADETTE. Please.

KIP. Your hair.

BERNADETTE. It's dirty.

KIP. It's perfect.

BERNADETTE. Let go.

KIP. You're beautiful.

BERNADETTE. I'm not.

KIP. To me.

BERNADETTE. You have . . .

KIP. You are.

BERNADETTE. Really lost your mind.

(*He kisses her. It quickly becomes passionate and they sink to the floor, making love. Fadeout.*)

COMMENTARY: Nicky Silver has written a screwball comedy dealing with the serious subjects of guilt, redemption and self-punishment. Kip and Bernadette hate their lives and feel imprisoned by their dysfunctional daily existence. They are both self-centred and egotistical, unwilling and unable to accommodate any opinions that contradict their own. The funeral of his hated mother-in-law proves to be a turning point for Kip. He realises he has been in denial for too long and finally finds the motivation to quit being a dentist. His decision is made easier by the knowledge that Bernadette will soon inherit money from her mother's estate. Notice how Kip's calm conviction comes into conflict with Bernadette's scepticism and scorn. He has experienced a life-enhancing breakthrough; she has not, and absolutely resists being caught up in his fanciful artistic enthusiasms. Despite the serious subject matter there is a darkly farcical quality to the writing – especially whenever teeth are mentioned – and this requires expert timing from the actors. There may be a temptation to make these characters too irritating but you must try to find a sympathetic core, otherwise you will instantly lose your audience's interest and attention.

Shopping and F***ing
Mark Ravenhill

Scene 2. Interview room. London.

For some time, Robbie and his companion, Lulu (both early 20s), have been living with Mark, a former wealthy city type, in a bizarre and sinister ménage à trois. Mark has taken the two of them under his wing, promising, 'I love you both and I want to look after you for ever and ever.' Since then, thanks to Mark's pay packet, they have enjoyed 'Good times. The three of us. Parties. Falling into taxis, out of taxis. Bed.' But Mark has now reached a crisis point where he has run out of money and lost his job. He decides to check himself into a drug rehabilitation centre. This leaves Lulu and Robbie to fend entirely for themselves. Lulu, who has trained as an actress, applies for a job as a TV presenter on a home shopping channel. Brian (late 30s) is the producer of the shopping programme. He is married and has a young son of whom he is extremely proud. It transpires that he pays for his son's private education and prized cello lessons with the money he makes by employing people like Lulu to sell Ecstasy at local raves. As this scene opens, Lulu is in the midst of her audition with Brian and she is completely unaware of his alternative agenda.

(BRIAN *and* LULU *sit facing each other.* BRIAN *is showing* LULU *an illustrated plastic plate.*)

BRIAN. And there's this moment. This really terrific moment. Quite possibly the best moment. Because really, you see, his father is dead. Yes? The father was crushed – you feel the sorrow welling up in you – crushed by a wild herd of these big cows. One moment, lord of all he surveys. And then . . . a breeze, a wind, the stamping of a

64

hundred feet and he's gone. Only it wasn't an accident. Somebody had a plan. You see?

LULU. Yes. I see.

BRIAN. Any questions. Any uncertainties. You just ask.

LULU. Of course.

BRIAN. Because I want you to follow.

LULU. Absolutely.

BRIAN. So then we're . . . there's . . .

LULU. Crushed by a herd of wild cows.

BRIAN. Crushed by a herd of wild cows. Yes.

LULU. Only it wasn't an accident.

BRIAN. Good. Excellent. Exactly. It wasn't an accident. It may have looked like an accident but – no. It was arranged by the uncle. Because –

LULU. Because he wanted to be King all along.

BRIAN. Thought you said you hadn't seen it.

LULU. I haven't.

Instinct. I have good instincts. That's one of my qualities. I'm an instinctive person.

BRIAN. Is that right?

(BRIAN *writes down 'instinctive' on a pad.*)

BRIAN. Good. Instinctive. Could be useful.

LULU. Although of course I can also use my rational side. Where appropriate.

BRIAN. So you'd say you appreciate order?

LULU. Order. Oh yes. Absolutely. Everything in its place.

(BRIAN *writes down 'appreciates order'.*)

BRIAN. Good. So now the father is dead. Murdered. It was the uncle. And the son has grown up. And you know – he looks like the dad. Just like him. And this sort of monkey thing comes to him. And this monkey says: 'It's time to speak to your dead dad.' So he goes to the stream and he looks in and he sees –

LULU. /His own reflection.

BRIAN. His own reflection. You've never seen this?

65

LULU. Never.

BRIAN. But then . . . The water ripples, it hazes. Until he sees a ghost. A ghost or a memory looking up at him. His . . .

(*Pause.*)

Excuse me. It takes you right here. Your throat tightens. Until . . . he sees . . . his . . . dad.

My little one. Gets to that bit and I look round and he's got these big tears in his eyes. He feels it like I do.

Because now the dad speaks. And he says: 'The time has come. It is time for you to take your place in the Cycle of Being (words to that effect). You are my son and the one true King.'

And he knows what it is he's got to do. He knows who it is he has to kill.

And that's the moment. That's our favourite bit.

LULU. I can see that. Yes.

BRIAN. Would you say you in any way resembled your father?

LULU. No. Not really. Not much.

BRIAN. Your mother?

LULU. Maybe. Sometimes. Yes.

BRIAN. You do know who your parents are?

LULU. Of course. We still . . . you know. Christmas. We spend Christmas together. On the whole.

(BRIAN *writes down 'celebrates Christmas'*.)

BRIAN. So many today are lost. Isn't that so?

LULU. I think that's right. Yes.

BRIAN. All they want is something.

And some come here. They look to me. You're looking to me aren't you?

Well aren't you?

LULU. Yes. I'm looking to you.

BRIAN (*proffers plate*). Here. Hold it. Just hold it up beside you. See if you look right. Smile. Look interested.

66

Because this is special. You wouldn't want to part with this. Can you give me that look?

(LULU *attempts the look*.)

BRIAN. That's good. Very good. Our viewers, they have to believe that what we hold up to them is special. For the right sum – life is easier, richer, more fulfilling. And you have to believe that too. Do you think you can do that?

(*Again* LULU *attempts the look*.)

BRIAN. Good. That's very good. We don't get many in your league.

LULU. Really?

BRIAN. No. That really is very . . . distinctive.

LULU. Well. Thank you. Thanks.

BRIAN. And now: 'Just a few more left. So dial this number now.'

LULU. Just a few more left. So dial this number now.

BRIAN. Excellent. Natural. Professional. Excellent.

LULU. I have had training.

BRIAN. So you're . . . ?

LULU. I'm a trained actor.

(BRIAN *writes down 'trained actor'*.)

BRIAN. I don't recognise you.

LULU. No? Well, probably not.

BRIAN. Do some for me now.

LULU. You want me to . . . ?

BRIAN. I want to see you doing some acting.

LULU. I didn't realise. I haven't prepared.

BRIAN. Come on. You're an actress. You must be able to do some acting.

An actress – if she can't do acting when she's asked, then what is she really?

She's nothing.

LULU. All right.

(LULU *stands up*.)

LULU. I haven't actually done this one before. In front of anyone.

BRIAN. Never mind. You're doing it now.

LULU. One day people will know what all this was for. All this suffering.

BRIAN. Take your jacket off.

LULU. I'm sorry?

BRIAN. I'm asking you to take your jacket off. Can't act with your jacket on.

LULU. Actually, I find it helps.

BRIAN. In what way?

LULU. The character.

BRIAN. Yes. But it's not helping me. I'm here to assess your talents and you're standing there acting in a jacket.

LULU. I'd like to keep it on.

BRIAN (*stands*). All right. I'll call the girl. Or maybe you remember the way?

LULU. No.

BRIAN. What do you mean – no?

LULU. I mean . . . please, I'd like this job. I want to be considered for this job.

BRIAN. Then we'll continue. Without the jacket. Yes?

(*LULU removes her jacket. Two chilled ready meals fall to the floor.*)

BRIAN. Look at all this.

(*They both go to pick up the meals. BRIAN gets there first.*)

BRIAN. Exotic.

LULU. We've got really into them. That's what we eat. For supper.

BRIAN. Did you pay for these?

LULU. Yes.

BRIAN. Stuffed into your jacket. Did you pay for them?

LULU. Yes.

BRIAN. Look me in the eyes. Did. You. Pay?

LULU. No.

68

BRIAN. Stolen goods.

LULU. We have to eat. We have to get by. I don't like this. I'm not a shoplifter. By nature. My instinct is for work. I need a job. Please.

BRIAN. You're an actress by instinct but theft is a necessity. Unless you can persuade me that I need you. All right. Carry on. Act a bit more.

No shirt.

LULU. No . . . ?

BRIAN. Carry on without the . . . (what's the . . . ?) . . . blouse.

(LULU *removes her blouse*.)

LULU. One day people will know what all this was for. All this suffering. There'll be no more mysteries. But until then we must carry on working. We must work. That's all we can do. I'm leaving by myself tomorrow . . .

BRIAN (*stifling a sob*). Oh, God.

LULU. I'm sorry. Shall I stop?

BRIAN. Carry on. As you were.

LULU. Leaving by myself tomorrow. I'll teach in a school and devote my whole life to people who need it. It's autumn now. It will soon be winter and there'll be snow everywhere. But I'll be working.

That's all.

(LULU *puts her shirt and jacket on*.)

BRIAN (*wipes away a tear*). Perfect. Brilliant. Did you make it up?

LULU. No. I learnt it. From a book.

BRIAN. Brilliant. So you think you can sell?

LULU. I know I can sell.

BRIAN. Because you're an actress?

LULU. It helps.

BRIAN. You seem very confident.

LULU. I am.

BRIAN. All right then. A trial. Something by way of a

test. I'm going to give you something to sell and we're
going to see how well you do. Clear so far?
LULU. Totally.
BRIAN. You understand that I am *entrusting* you?
LULU. I understand.
BRIAN. I am entrusting you to pass this important test.
LULU. I'm not going to let you down.
BRIAN. Good.
(BRIAN *reaches for his briefcase and starts to open it.*)

COMMENTARY: This darkly comic drama presents a desolate
world in which sex, drugs and junk food take precedence over
relationships and conventional morality. The two characters in
this scene are both obsessed and desperate, but in quite
different ways. At this point in the play, Lulu seems prepared to
do anything to make some money and Brian exploits her
eagerness and vulnerability. When Brian asks Lulu to take off
her top she is more concerned that her stolen heat-and-serve
meals will drop out from under her jacket than she is about
revealing her breasts. Do you think Brian ever really intended to
offer Lulu a job or is the interview merely a front? Brian's
interview technique is somewhat unorthodox and has the
intensity of an interrogation. Brian is a consummate manipula-
tor whose smarmy manner is tingled with an aura of menace.
There is something comically sinister in his obsession with *The
Lion King*. For this scene to work in performance you must find
a way to make your audience both laugh and squirm. This scene
starts in the middle of the conversation between Lulu and
Brian; how do you think they got to this point?

Simpatico
Sam Shepard

Act 3, scene 1. Living room of Carter's Kentucky mansion, very simple set with the impression of wealth.

Vinnie (40s) is 'dressed in a dark blue long-sleeved shirt, dark slacks with no belt. Everything very rumpled as though he's been sleeping in his clothes for weeks . . . with a "Redwing" shoebox tucked under his arm.' Rosie (late 30s) is 'slightly hung over and rumpled'. She is still wearing her robe. Rosie's husband, Carter, and Vinnie have known each other since they were kids. Fifteen years ago they were business partners involved in a California racetrack scam that involved the swapping of two racehorses and the gross sexual blackmail of Simms, the local commissioner of racing. Vinnie still holds the vital evidence that could incriminate his one-time partner and over the years Carter has paid Vinnie to keep him quiet. At the time of the scam Vinnie and Rosie were married but she then eloped with Carter and married him. Vinnie and Rosie have not seen each other since that time. Rosie now leads a life of wealth and comfort with a nanny to look after her two children. Over the years, as Carter has prospered as a horse breeder, Vinnie has become an increasingly reclusive bum, indulging in fantasy detective games. Vinnie summons Carter to his rundown apartment in Cucamonga in California. He lures him with the pretence that he needs his help to deal with a 'major crisis' involving a girlfriend who had him arrested for assault. However, it transpires that Vinnie has decided that the time has come to revenge himself on Carter and this is all part of his warped plot. In this scene, having abandoned Carter in Cucamonga, Vinnie comes unannounced to Carter's house to visit Rosie. This is their first encounter in fifteen years.

ROSIE. Would you like me to take your coat and uh – your package?

VINNIE. No thanks.

ROSIE. If you're wearing a sidearm under there it doesn't matter. We've seen that before around here. Kelly's seen it. It's old hat.

VINNIE. I'm not.

ROSIE. So, you haven't come to do me in then? Splatter my brains all over the carpet in a fit of jealous rage? (*Pause.*) You're a long way from home, Vinnie.

VINNIE. Yeah. I am.

ROSIE. Carter just went out to see you. Did you know that? That's what he said he was up to anyway. You didn't somehow miss him did you? 'Ships in the night'?

VINNIE. No. I saw him.

ROSIE. Oh, good. Did you work things out? I know it's been a long and bitter negotiation.

VINNIE. He said you two were on the outs.

ROSIE. Who?

VINNIE. You and him.

ROSIE (*laughs*). Is that what he said? Just like that? 'On the outs'! Those were *his* words?

(*Pause*).

VINNIE. Is it okay if I – sit down?

ROSIE. Help yourself! *Mi casa es su casa*, Vinnie. You know that. Just like the old days. Nothing's changed.

(VINNIE *sits on edge of sofa, clutching shoebox under his arm.*)

ROSIE. So, what've you got, a bomb in the box or something? Gonna blow us all to Kingdom Come?

VINNIE. I'm not going to hurt you.

ROSIE. You're not still harboring something, are you Vinnie? That's not healthy. That's the kind of thing that leads to cancer and insanity.

VINNIE. I just wanted to see you.

ROSIE. Well, here I am! Still in the bloom of things. I never would've recognized *you* though, Vinnie. You've let yourself go. I was watching you from the window and I was asking myself, 'Now who is this? Who in the world could this be, arriving by taxi, with a package under his arm?' It's not roses, is it, Vinnie? Roses for Rosie?

VINNIE. No.

ROSIE. I didn't think so. Too short for roses. Too compact. Unless you've cut the stems off. Out of spite or something. Wouldn't that be a shame.

VINNIE. So, how did you know?

ROSIE. What.

VINNIE. How did you recognize me?

ROSIE. Oh. The voice. Something in the voice rang a bell. A kind of apologetic menace. I don't know how else to describe it.

VINNIE. I'm not going to hurt you.

ROSIE. I'd feel a lot more reassured if you didn't keep repeating that.

VINNIE. I just want you to know. I didn't come here for that.

ROSIE. Good. That's good news. Now we don't have to talk about it anymore, do we? (*Pause.*) So you met up with Carter then? How did that go?

VINNIE. All right.

ROSIE. He said you were in some kind of an emergency again. He left here in a big rush.

VINNIE. I am.

ROSIE. Still?

VINNIE. Yes. I'm at the end of my rope. I may not look like it but I am.

ROSIE. Well, actually, you *are* looking a little rough around the edges, Vinnie. I didn't want to say anything –

VINNIE. I got arrested.

ROSIE. Oh. That's too bad. When was that?

73

VINNIE. A while back. Couple weeks ago.

ROSIE. Well, I'm sorry to hear that, Vinnie. What was it this time?

VINNIE. Assault with a deadly weapon. Attempted manslaughter.

ROSIE. You've escalated.

VINNIE. It won't stick. Just – hysterical reaction, is all it was.

ROSIE. It wasn't Carter, was it?

VINNIE. What.

ROSIE. Did you assault Carter?

VINNIE. No. He's safe.

ROSIE. Where is he?

VINNIE. Out there. My place.

ROSIE. How come he's out there and you're here? What's going on, Vinnie?

VINNIE. He's – He took up with a woman out there.

[(*Pause*. ROSIE *stares at him*. KELLY *re-enters with a tray and drinks. Pause, as she sets the drinks down on glass table then turns to go.* ROSIE *stops her.*)

ROSIE. Kelly?

KELLY (*stops*). Yes, mam?

ROSIE. What time are you picking up the kids today?

KELLY. Three o'clock. The usual time.

ROSIE. Doesn't Simon have band practice?

KELLY. No, not today. That's Thursdays.

ROSIE. Oh. Right. Well, look, Kelly, why don't you take them to have ice cream and then go to Toys 'R' Us or something. All right? Just find something to do with them for a little while.

KELLY (*looks at* VINNIE). Okay.

ROSIE. I need to talk with Mr Webb here.

KELLY. All right.

(KELLY *starts to go, then stops. She eyes* VINNIE *then turns to* ROSIE.)

74

KELLY (*to* ROSIE). Is everything – Are you sure you'll be all right, Mrs Carter?

ROSIE. I'm fine, Kelly. Just go get the kids now. Do as you're told.

(KELLY *eyes* VINNIE *again, then exits. Pause as* ROSIE *and* VINNIE *sip their drinks.*)]

ROSIE. So – he's run off with a woman. Not that I'm shocked or anything. He's been carrying on behind my back since day one.

VINNIE. When *was* that?

ROSIE. What?

VINNIE. 'Day One'.

ROSIE. We're not going to drag that back up out of the dirt, are we, Vinnie? Things happened. One thing led to another. I don't know. It was a long time ago.

VINNIE. But now it's over, right?

ROSIE. What.

VINNIE. You and him?

ROSIE. Apparently so! What're you trying to tell me? He's shacked up with a woman at *your* place and you've come all the way out here to give me the good news?

VINNIE. He met this girl –

ROSIE. A girl! A girl! It's always a girl. Never a woman.

VINNIE. He met this girl in a bar out there.

ROSIE. What a surprise!

VINNIE. I guess she got infatuated with him.

ROSIE. Oh, *she* got infatuated with *him*!

VINNIE. I guess.

ROSIE. And you, very generously, donated your bed to the cause!

VINNIE. No –

ROSIE. And now you've gone out of your way, as a friend, to make sure I understand all the sordid details!

VINNIE (*sudden burst*). HE STOLE MY BUICK,

75

ROSIE! HE STOLE MY BUICK AND HE STOLE MY WIFE!

(*Pause.* ROSIE *stares at him.*)

ROSIE. You know, for a long time I kept dreading this confrontation. I had little nightmares about it. But now that it's here, it seems dull actually. Stupid.

VINNIE. You could've left me a note or something.

ROSIE. A note!

VINNIE. Something.

ROSIE. Oh you mean like: 'Gone to the 7–11 to get a six-pack. Be right back'?

VINNIE. Something. Not just – disappeared.

ROSIE. We were *all* checking out of there, Vinnie! *All* of us. That was the plan. Remember?

VINNIE. Yeah. I remember.

ROSIE. No contact. No trace of any connection between us.

VINNIE. That was the plan.

ROSIE. It's a little late for regrets.

VINNIE. I just thought maybe you'd –

ROSIE. What?

(*Pause.*)

VINNIE. Come back.

ROSIE. To what? Life on the backstretch? Fifteen-hundred-dollar claimers? I could've set up house in the back of a horse trailer, maybe?

VINNIE. We had fun. We had some fun.

ROSIE. Fun!

VINNIE. Read the Form 'til two in the morning sometimes. Picking long-shots. Clocking works.

ROSIE. Fun.

VINNIE. Slept in the truck bed. Listened to the tin roof flap on that shedrow.

ROSIE. Fun, fun, fun!

VINNIE. You could've called me or something.

76

ROSIE. What about *you*? Where have you been all this time?

VINNIE. I had no idea where you went.

ROSIE. Come on. You knew where the checks were coming from. You knew the phone number well enough.

VINNIE. I didn't want to – interrupt your life.

ROSIE. Get outa here.

VINNIE. I thought you and Carter were –

ROSIE. What.

VINNIE. Getting along. I mean –

ROSIE. *You're* the one who disappeared, Vinnie. *You're* the one who vanished.

VINNIE. I'm here, now.

ROSIE. Well, isn't that great! Isn't that dandy! Fifteen years later you sneak through my back door with a dumb box and a hang-dog look on your face.

VINNIE. I wasn't sneaking.

ROSIE. What'd you come here for?
(*Pause.*)
VINNIE. I thought maybe I could set things straight.

COMMENTARY: In *Simpatico* Shepard portrays the dissolution of the American dream into a web of lies, corruption and rootless frenzy. Vinnie is a loner fuelled by vindictive vengeance. He is festering with a deep sense of betrayal and isolation and he wants his retribution now. Why do you think he has waited so long to confront Carter? For Vinnie the past overshadows the present. Vinnie, in his warped plan, aims to play on Carter's guilt and fear. What does he really want to get from black-mailing Carter and confronting Rosie. Imagine how Vinnie's pent-up rage and menace have distorted his grasp of reality. Over the years Vinnie's obsession with Rosie has grown as has his sense of betrayal and resentment towards Rosie and Carter. Rosie now leads a cosseted but washed-up existence; like a character from Sartre, she is locked in a hell of her own making. In this scene the audience does not yet know what is in Vinnie's box and why earlier in the play Carter was so eager to get his hands on it. For the actors in this scene it is important that they know that Rosie was involved in the sexual scam that destroyed Simms: she was the trick who was photographed in explicitly sexual photos which Vinnie has stored away in his shoebox over the years. You must retain an incredible tension between the two characters; both verbal and physical violence are just beneath the surface. For Rosie, Vinnie is the last person in the world she wants to see and her sardonic disdain makes him keep his distance. Vinnie tries to provoke her but she just will not be drawn into his frenzy of retribution.

Some Voices
Joe Penhall

Act 1, scene 6. A pub in Shepherd's Bush, west London.

Laura is in her early twenties, Irish and unemployed. She is pregnant by Dave, her possessive thug of a boyfriend. Ray is also in his twenties. In the week following his release from a mental hospital, where he was treated for schizophrenia, he has been living with his older brother, Pete. The hospital has prescribed heavy medication to stabilise his erratic behaviour and mood swings. However Ray, unbeknownst to Pete, stops taking his pills. Pete is harassed and overworked running his restaurant, and he ends up leaving Ray to his own devices. In an earlier scene, Dave grills Laura about the whereabouts of a ring he gave her, arguing that she must have given it to her 'fancy man'. When she flatly denies this, insisting that she has just lost it, Dave starts to beat her up. At this point Ray (who has never met either Dave or Laura before) innocently walks by and tries to intervene to save Laura. Dave wrongly assumes that Ray is Laura's 'fancy man' and then viciously beats him up. Laura ends up taking Ray back to her bedsit where she quickly cleans up his injuries and then sends him packing. In this scene, a couple of days later, Ray finds Laura again in a local pub.

(LAURA *is sitting at a table drinking and smoking a cigarette. Music blasts out.* RAY *wanders over with drink in hand.*)
RAY. Is . . . anybody sitting there?
LAURA. Only if they're very small.
RAY. Can I sit there?
(LAURA *shrugs.* RAY *sits.*)
RAY. All right?
(*Pause.*)

79

It's nice here. (*Beat.*) All my friends come here. (*Beat.*) They're not here at the moment.

LAURA. I like it.

RAY. It's a friendly place. I like the music they play. It's not old and it's not new. Very few pubs play this type of music nowadays. Are you Irish?

LAURA. What?

RAY. This is an Irish pub.

LAURA. I'm from Limerick.

RAY. Did you know that there is more drunkenness, suicide and madness amongst the Irish in London than any other race on earth?

LAURA. Is that so?

RAY. Yes, well, that's what they say because mostly you see they're away from their family and they're lonely probably and sometimes there's prejudice against 'em because of who they are and they can't get jobs and things but also mainly it's just loneliness. Have you got any family here or are you just on your own?

LAURA. I'm on my own.

RAY. Me too. I just got my brother. Me dad vanished some years ago but there's still my brother. My mother's dead. Cancer I believe.

(*Pause.*)

No cats, no dogs, no – what are they – little hairy things, in a cage ... I don't have any sisters. Do you have any sisters?

LAURA. Yeh, I've got a couple of sisters.

RAY. And do you like them?

LAURA. They're all right.

RAY. That's good because you have to be able to like your family. You have to be able to trust them but mainly you have to like them. And sometimes you just don't. Sometimes you don't trust anybody. Then again sometimes you form a vague attachment/to –

LAURA. I have no idea, no idea at all, what you are talking about. Can you see that?

(*Pause.*)

RAY. Would you like a drink?

LAURA. Look, I'm sorry if it looked like I wanted you to sit down but in fact I really didn't. What I wanted was to be left alone. And I'm not just saying that, I mean it. I don't want to talk to anybody I don't want to see anybody I don't want to fight with anybody I don't want to drink with anybody smile at anybody play Let's Get To Know Each Other I just don't want to know. I'm in a bad mood.

RAY. Well, why'd you come here?

LAURA. Because . . . I'm in a bad mood. Why did you come here?

RAY (*beat*). I was bored.

LAURA. You were bored so you thought you'd come and talk to me.

(RAY *shrugs. Pause.*)

RAY. It's nice here. I live round here. My brother he runs a restaurant it's very busy, sometimes I help out.

LAURA. Really.

RAY. Yes, all the time. (*Beat.*) No, never. What happened to your face?

LAURA. What?

RAY. You/all right?

LAURA. Nothing happened.

RAY. That doesn't look like nothing to me. You got quite a shiner. And your lip's all cut. And your arm, look at your arm.

LAURA. I fell out of bed.

RAY. Ah, I'm always falling out of bed. Falling out of bed and walking into doors. You want to get some carpet in that place that way you won't bruise so easy. So so so did you get to your appointment?

(LAURA *looks at him then glances around the pub uneasily.*)

LAURA. Yes, thank you.

RAY. You must be up the spout then. Am I right?

LAURA. I beg your pardon?

RAY. Is it his then? That fella of yours?

LAURA. Yes it's his all his handiwork just like your nose. Any other/questions?

RAY. I'm surprised people still want to have babies. I find it fascinating. I mean they say you get a special glow and everything when you have a baby. Like a special . . .

(*She gets up.*)

LAURA. I have to go.

RAY. Please stay, sit down don't get all –

(RAY *gets up and puts a hand on her arm, she bats it away.*)

LAURA. Don't touch me!

RAY. Sorry!

LAURA. What is wrong with you?

RAY. I just want to get to know you a bit, what's wrong with that?

LAURA. You don't get to know somebody by just walking up to them in a pub and talking absolute friggin' rubbish to them for half an hour.

RAY. What d'you want me to do?

LAURA. Are you simple or wha'?

RAY. I offered you a drink.

LAURA. That is not how it happens.

RAY. Well, how does it happen?

LAURA. I don't know!

RAY. You don't believe me, do you? I like you. I'm not being funny. I thought you liked me seeing as I saved your life and all. I can't do that every day you know, my brother ain't half got the hump. He don't believe me neither.

(*Pause.* LAURA *sighs and sits.*)

RAY. You got nice eyes.

LAURA. I don't believe this.

RAY. Incredible blue like two swimming pools.

82

LAURA. You don't give up, do you?

RAY. Not really/no.

LAURA. I'm not going to sleep with you, you know.

RAY. What?

LAURA. I said . . . (*Lowers her voice.*) I'm not going to sleep with you. If that's what you're getting at.

RAY. I don't want you to sleep with me.

LAURA. It's out of the question.

RAY. I didn't ask you to sleep/with me.

LAURA. Because, because –

RAY. I don't want you to sleep/with me.

LAURA. I'm not sleeping with/anybody.

RAY. I don't want you/to.

LAURA. Just at the moment. Sleeping with people is not the answer to/anything.

RAY. I don't want you to sleep with me.

(*Pause.*)

LAURA. And I'm not doing anything else either.

RAY. I don't want you to.

LAURA. Nothing, you understand? Nothing.

RAY. I don't want to.

(*Pause. They look around sheepishly.*)

LAURA. Well, good. I'm glad we got that sorted/out.

RAY. Who said anything about sleeping with you?

LAURA. I just thought that might have been where things were heading.

RAY. Course not. (*Beat.*) I don't like sleeping anyway, it's boring. I've been asleep for too long.

LAURA. You know that's not what/I meant.

RAY. I can't sleep, at night my brother says, 'Go to sleep,' and I can't. I don't want to. I have nightmares.

(*Pause.*)

LAURA. What d'you have nightmares about?

RAY. Strange things. Things are always the wrong colour

83

or the wrong size. Things speaking to me. Like birds. I mean real birds that fly.

LAURA. What's so scary about that? I'd love to have nightmares about birds.

RAY. I scare easily. Well, I can't speak to them, can I? I'm not Doctor fuckin' Doolittle. (*Beat. She laughs a little.*) What about yours?

LAURA. Who said I get 'em?

RAY. You must do.

LAURA. Yeh, well . . . I wake up before anything really bad happens.

RAY. I know that sort and all. Awful.

LAURA. Yeh . . . awful.

(*Pause.*)

I'm/sorry I –

RAY. No, I'm/sorry.

LAURA. I didn't/mean to –

RAY. I just barged/in –

LAURA. No you –

RAY. I –

LAURA. I –

RAY. I'll get the drinks in.

LAURA. Get the drinks in good idea.

RAY. A pint is it?

LAURA. Vodka. Double.

(RAY *gets up hurriedly and goes to the bar.* LAURA *smokes her cigarette. Pause. She fidgets.* RAY *returns and plonks a vodka orange and a beer down.*)

RAY. You shouldn't smoke and drink you know.

LAURA. There's a lot of things I shouldn't do.

RAY. But you still do 'em. Me too. I personally like to live as if I'm gonna die tomorrow.

LAURA. You might do.

RAY. Yeh, yes that's exactly it. That's exactly it.

(*Pause.*)

84

I'm Ray, by the way.

LAURA. Laura.

(*He puts his hand out, they shake. Beat.*)

RAY. Can I have a feel?

LAURA. What?

RAY. Of your . . . of the . . .

(*He indicates her belly.*)

LAURA. Of this?

(RAY *nods.* RAY *puts his hand on her belly.* LAURA *looks straight ahead.* RAY *puts his ear to her belly and listens.* LAURA *looks around awkwardly.*)

COMMENTARY: This is a bleakly comic play about schizophrenia. Ray has been released from the closeted safety of the asylum into a nightmare world full of rage and madness. He is a figure of troubled charm, displaying an innocent chivalry towards Laura. The actor playing Ray must allow the knowledge of his schizophrenia to inform his performance without telegraphing a 'mad' or 'crazy' demeanour. His illness manifests itself in a gentle boyishness and an engaging verbosity. Ray is a sensitive, pleasant lad tortured by his illness but determined to prove his own resilience. Laura also displays a strong resilient streak; but why do you think she allows Dave repeatedly to abuse her? She is wary of Ray and reacts to him with a mixture of compassion and prickly defensiveness. Laura has a deep sense of fear and pain which makes her wary of Ray's 'friendly' overtures. The actor playing Laura must be careful to balance her obvious irritation with Ray with a genuine tenderness.

Two
Jim Cartwright

One Act. A pub in the north of England.

Moth (40) comes to the pub before his girlfriend Maudie (late 30s).
He is a compulsive flirt and drives Maudie to distraction. Maudie
yearns desperately for commitment in their relationship but Moth is
reluctant to settle down. Moth is permanently broke and relies on
Maudie to subsidise his life. She is patient and long-suffering. While
waiting for Maudie, he is trying to chat up a girl at the bar. As this
scene begins his attempted seduction is interrupted by Maudie's
arrival.

(MAUDIE *has entered and taps him on the shoulder.*)
MAUDIE. Hiyah Moth.
MOTH. What are you doing here?
MAUDIE. I'm your bleeding bird aren't I?
MOTH (*looking round*). Yes, yes, but . . .
MAUDIE. Moth. Moth she wasn't interested.
MOTH. How do you know that?
MAUDIE. Believe me I know. Moth, Moth do you still
love me?
MOTH. Of course I do, get them in.
MAUDIE. No, I'm not this time.
MOTH. Eh?
MAUDIE. I've had a good talking to by some of the girls
at work today. And they've told me once and for all. I've
not to let you keep using me.
MOTH. Using. Using. You sing and I'll dance. Ha! No
Maudie you know that's not me. But when I'm broke what
86

can I do, I depend on those that say they love me to care for me. And anyway it's always been our way.

MAUDIE. Stop. Stop now. Don't keep turning me over with your tongue.

MOTH. Maudie, my Maudie.

(*He takes her in his arms, kisses her. She swoons.*)

MAUDIE. Oh here get the drinks in.

MOTH (*he opens handbag*). Ah that sweet click. (*Takes out some money.*) Here I go.

(*He sets off around the other side of bar to get served.*)

MAUDIE. Oh no. No. Look he's off with my money again . . . I said this wouldn't happen again and here it is, happened. I've got to get me some strength. Where is it? (*Makes a fist and twists it.*) Ah there. Hold that Maudie. Maudie, Maudie hold that.

(MOTH *on his way back with the drinks. Bumps into someone. Dolly bird.*)

MOTH. Oops sorry love. Bumpsadaisy. You all right . . .

MAUDIE. Moth!

MOTH. See you. Better get these over to me sister. (*Passing others.*) 'Scuse me. (*Others.*) Yep yep. (*Others.*) Beep beep. Here we go Maud.

MAUDIE. What were you . . . (*Shows fist to* MOTH.)

MOTH (*giving drink*). And here's your speciality.

MAUDIE. Aww you always get it just right. Nobody gets it like you. The ice, the umbrella.

MOTH. Of course. Of course.

(MAUDIE *kisses him.*)

MAUDIE. Oh look. I'm going again. All over you.

MOTH. That's all right, just watch the shirt.

(*They drink. He begins looking around. She looks at him looking around. She makes the fist again.*)

MAUDIE. Look at me will you. Look at your eyes, they're everywhere, up every skirt, along every leg, round every bra rim. Why oh why do you keep chasing women!

87

MOTH. Oh we're not going to have to go through all this again are we petal. Is this the girls at work priming you?

MAUDIE. Yes a bit, no a bit. I don't know. I can't remember now, so much has been said. I just want you to stop it.

MOTH. But you know I can't stop myself.

MAUDIE. But you never even get off with them.

MOTH. I know.

MAUDIE. It's like the girls say, I hold all the cards.

MOTH. How do you mean?

MAUDIE. I'm the only woman on earth interested in you.

MOTH. Well yes, but . . .

MAUDIE. Moth let it all go and let's get settled down.

MOTH. I can't it's something I've always done and I guess I always will. (*Again looking at some women.*)

MAUDIE. No, Moth, no . . . Oh how can I get it through to you.

MOTH (*draining his glass empty*). Drink by drink.

MAUDIE. No way. Buzz off Moth.

MOTH. Come on love, get them in. Let's have a few and forget all this. You pay, I'll order.

MAUDIE. No.

MOTH. But Maudie, my Maudie.

MAUDIE. No, I'm stopping the tap. I shall not be used.

MOTH. Used. Used. Well if that's how you feel I can always go you know.

(*He walks down the bar a bit, stops, looks back, walks down the bar a bit, stops, looks back. Falls over a stool. Picks it up, laughs to cover embarrassment, limps back to her.*)

Maudie, I've been thinking, all what you're saying's so true and right as always. I'm losing everything, my flair, my waistline, what's next to go – you? Will it be you next?

MAUDIE (*unmoved*). You'll try anything won't you, just to get into my handbag. The romantic approach, the comic approach, the concern for me approach, the sympathy approach. Does it never end?

MOTH. You forgot sexy in there.

(*She swings for him, he ducks.*)

No Maudie. You're right again. What does a princess like you see in a loser like me?

MAUDIE. I don't know. Well I do. You're romantic, like something on the fade. I love that.

MOTH (*moving in*). Oh Maudie, my Maudie.

(*As he does, she starts to melt again, he starts to reach into her handbag, she suddenly sees this and slams it shut on his hand.*)

MAUDIE. Stop!

MOTH. Aw Maud. How can I prove I'm genuine to you? Here take everything on me, everything, everything. (*Starts frantically emptying his pockets.*) My last 10p, I'm going to give it to you!

MAUDIE. I don't want your poxy ten.

MOTH. You say that now, you say that now Maud, but you don't know what it's going to turn into. I'm going to give you all I've got left. My final, last and only possession. (*Spins and drops it in jukebox.*) My dancing talent.

('*Kiss*' *by Tom Jones comes on.* MOTH *dances.*)

MOTH. 'Cause Maud, whatever you say. Whatever's said and done. I'm still a top dancer 'ant I hey?

MAUDIE. Well you can move.

MOTH. I can Maud. I sure as hell can Maud. (*Dancing.*) I'm dancing for you Maudie. For you only. (*Dancing.*) Come on get up here with me.

(*She comes to him, puts her handbag on the floor, they dance.*)

MOTH. Who's lost it all now eh?

(*He really grooves it.*)

MAUDIE (*worried, embarrassed*). Moth.

MOTH. Come on doll.

MAUDIE. Moth take it easy.

MOTH. Come on. Swing it. Let your backbone slip.

89

Yeah let your . . . Awwwwwww Ow ow!!! (*Stops. Can't move.*)

MAUDIE. Moth, oh God, what is it?

MOTH. Me back, me back. Help oh help.

MAUDIE. What can I do! What can I do!

MOTH. Get me a chair, get me a gin.

MAUDIE (*feeling up his back*). Where is it? Where is it?

MOTH. There between the whiskey and the vodka.

MAUDIE. Ooo another trick, you snide, you emperor of snide! (*Hits him.*)

MOTH. No, no Maud. Really, you've got it all wrong. It's real. Arwwwwww. Get me to a chair!

MAUDIE. It's real is it you swine?

MOTH. Real. Real.

MAUDIE. Real is it?

MOTH (*nodding*). Arrgh. Arrgh.

MAUDIE. Okay let's test it.

MOTH. How?

(*She takes out a fiver and holds it in front of him. He tries to go for it, but he can't.*)

MAUDIE (*amazed*). It is true. (*Starts circling him.*) Trapped. At last after all these years, I finally have that fluttering Moth pinned down. Ha.

MOTH. Oh Maudie what you gonna do?

MAUDIE. Let's see. Let's see here.

MOTH. Don't muck about how. I'm dying here, arrrgh, dying.

MAUDIE. So if, if, I help, what do I get out of it?

MOTH. Anything! Anything!

MAUDIE. Anything, anything eh?

MOTH. Yes, yes, arrrrgh.

MAUDIE. Okay, make an honest woman of me now.

MOTH. No, never, arrrr.

MAUDIE. Okay, see you love.

MOTH. No. Don't go Maud please.

MAUDIE. Sorry love, have to, love to stay but . . . 'bye. And any of you try to help him, you'll have me to deal with, and my handbag.

(MAUDIE *blows him a kiss as she goes. Exits.*)

MOTH. MAUD! Will you marry me?

MAUDIE (*coming back*). Sorry?

MOTH. Will you marry me?

MAUDIE. YES! OH YESSSSSSSSS! (*She comes running to him and hugs him.*)

MOTH (*she's hurt his back*). AARRRRGHHHH!

MAUDIE. Oh sorry love.

(*Still in embrace she guides him to a stool.*)

MOTH. A a aa a.

(*She props him against stool and bar, he is stiff like a board.*)

MOTH. Ah.

MAUDIE. Oh. Oh. (*Cuddling him.*) Oh. (*Suddenly serious.*) Do you still mean it?

MOTH. I mean it. I mean it. Singleness is all over for me.

MAUDIE (*hugging him again as best she can*). Oh Moth you won't regret this.

MOTH. Arrgh. I know. I know.

MAUDIE. I'll get us a taxi. Hold on now. Be brave. You poor thing.

(*She rushes out.*)

MOTH (*turns to girl at front*). You're beautiful you. Look at you. You're fantastic you.

(*Blackout.*)

COMMENTARY: Each scene in this poignantly comic play captures a host of characters as they pass through their local pub. The playwright reveals very little about each of these personalities. Moth is a down-market Don Juan. He flutters around women who attract him like a flame. He thinks of himself as a youthful Casanova, but in this scene he discovers he's creaky and middle-aged. He's got what he thinks is a very good line in romantic banter and chat-up lines. Maudie likes to think she is immune to all this; she's heard it a hundred times before and is not going to be seduced by his 'tongue'. She is down-to-earth, knows what she wants and speaks her mind. This evening she has come to the pub resolved once and for all to issue an ultimatum to Moth. But notice that as soon as Moth comes on to her with his romantic ways she 'swoons' and gives in to him. Maudie keeps trying to rally herself to her cause and cut Moth off each time he goes for her purse strings. To make this scene really effective you must find a subtle balance between the comedy and a genuine feeling for the plight of both Maudie and Moth.

The Woman Who Cooked Her Husband
Debbie Isitt

Scene 5. Hilary and Kenneth's house somewhere near Liverpool, England.

Hilary (40s) 'is dressed in a green taffeta outfit, green tights and shoes. She wears her hair in a beehive.' She is an expert cook and homemaker. Her husband, Kenneth (40s), is an ageing Teddy boy with a passion for Elvis Presley. 'His costume is a green taffeta drape coat with black drainpipe trousers.' After nineteen years of marriage, Kenneth embarks on a secret affair with Laura. He is terrified of approaching middle age and this affair makes him feel that 'I can put it off for a good few years, I'm starting again and I feel just like a teenager'. Laura has been pushing Kenneth to leave Hilary, but he wants to wait until the time is 'right'. At the same time, Hilary is beginning to suspect that Kenneth might be having an affair, but when she confronts him he strenuously denies this. Eventually Laura decides to have a showdown with Hilary. Their emotional confrontation (which can be found on page 178 of this volume) ends with Laura announcing that Kenneth is leaving Hilary in favour of Laura. This scene follows soon after as Kenneth arrives home completely oblivious of the drama that has just ensued.

KENNETH. Hi Hilary – I'm home – what's cooking?

HILARY. Have you had a good day at work?

KENNETH. Yep! What about you?

HILARY. I've had a great day.

KENNETH. How come?

HILARY. No reason. I just had a really great day.

KENNETH. What's for dinner? I'm starving.

HILARY. Nothing . . . I'll do you a salad.

93

KENNETH (*searching*). Where's my album?

HILARY. What album?

KENNETH. My *Aloha Hawaii* album.

HILARY. I don't know.

KENNETH. You don't know? Come on, you've spent the day tidying up, you must have moved it.

HILARY. I haven't touched it Kenneth.

KENNETH. Bloody hell!

HILARY. Did anything interesting happen to you today?

KENNETH. What do you mean, 'interesting'? What sort of question is that? What are you getting at with your 'interesting'?

HILARY. Nothing. I like to hear what you get up to.

KENNETH. What's 'get up to'? Why would I want to 'get up' to anything? It's work, a job – what's the matter with you?

HILARY. Nothing's the matter with me.

KENNETH. Always asking weird questions – why don't you just get off my back.

(*Pause.*)

HILARY. Your album's in the bin.

KENNETH. What?

HILARY. I trod on it. It cracked – I threw it in the bin.

KENNETH. For God's sake, woman, that's my best record!

HILARY. You should have put it away.

KENNETH. What's wrong with you, can't you watch where you're putting your big feet?

HILARY. Yes.

KENNETH. On top of everything else now you're accident-prone.

HILARY. It wasn't an accident.

KENNETH. You did it on purpose.

HILARY. Yes.

KENNETH. What do you mean?

94

HILARY. I trod on your stupid record on purpose.

KENNETH. You broke my record – on purpose!!?

HILARY. I JUST SAID SO, DIDN'T I?

KENNETH. You've got to be joking – people don't go around breaking my things for no reason.

HILARY. I'm not people, I'm your wife, and I had a good reason.

KENNETH. Why?

HILARY. I don't like it.

KENNETH. What?

HILARY. The record. It gets on my nerves.

KENNETH. You don't go around breaking other people's records just because they get on your nerves.

HILARY. I do.

KENNETH. Right. Give me the money.

HILARY. No.

KENNETH. Give me the money to buy a new one.

HILARY. No – get lost.

KENNETH. YOU are completely mental – I can't believe it.

HILARY. Why are you home so late?

KENNETH. The traffic was bad, why do you think? You break my record, you haven't cooked dinner, you give me the third degree on what I do every minute of the day – God knows why I married you.

(*Pause.*)

HILARY. I saw Laura today.

(*Pause. In the background, the Rossini Overture plays, indicating KENNETH's emotional panic.*)

KENNETH. Who?

HILARY. Laura – you don't know her. Someone I met once at a party.

KENNETH. Oh yeah? What, like an old friend?

HILARY. Not really a friend. More an acquaintance.

KENNETH. Yeah? . . . And?

HILARY. Nothing.

KENNETH. Nothing?

HILARY. Nothing.

KENNETH. Fine.

HILARY. How long has it been going on?

KENNETH. What?

HILARY. How long?

KENNETH. I don't know what you're talking about.

HILARY. It could have been going on for years.

KENNETH. WHAT!?

HILARY. You could have been sleeping with me, eating with me, pretending to be faithful to me for years and years – you might at least let me know when it started.

KENNETH. Please, Hilary – I don't know what you mean.

(HILARY *begins pushing him out of her side of the house. He walks backwards, tripping up the steps, refusing to be forced out.*)

HILARY. Have there been any others? Come on, let's hear it, how many have you slipped it into?

KENNETH. Eh . . .

HILARY. Why, Kenneth? Is it my body that repulses you? My personality? The way I speak – what?

KENNETH. You're – you're . . . hysterical! You don't know what you're saying.

HILARY. Hysterical? I'm not hysterical . . . I want you out. Out of this house tonight – I want you to get out and stay out – you can pack a bag and that's all – you take nothing – do you hear – nothing – everything in this house is mine, it's mine – it's all I've got and I'm keeping it – you've got her – now go . . .

(*During the following dialogue – until the blackout – the Rossini Overture increases in volume until it drowns out their voices so we only see the hysteria as she shouts at him to go.*)

KENNETH. Go where?

96

HILARY. Now Kenneth – quick.

KENNETH. But I don't know what you mean? Have you been drinking?

HILARY. You're a very sad man – very sad.

KENNETH. You can't just throw me out on the street – what am I supposed to have done? You haven't even told me what I've done.

HILARY. Go!

KENNETH. If this is about Laura – I do know a Laura, but nothing's gone on between us – why won't you just talk to me? I hardly know her – there's no way I would have –

HILARY. Just – get – out – of – my – house.

KENNETH. You'll feel different tomorrow – I'll call round.

HILARY. How could you – how could you!?

COMMENTARY: This play portrays a high-energy emotional journey. The playwright suggests in her foreword that each character 'has its own route and the action flares when the paths are crossed. Most of the work should be done out of the scene, building up the emotional truth ready to enter the scene so that the actors can just "be" there during the scene . . . The play should be served up at a fast, furious pace with savage emotional input, clear fast thought changes and an innocence that keeps the play alive and real . . . Dialogue exchanged with wit and passion . . . but never completely hiding the pain that runs very deep amongst all three characters.' Hilary has had some time to mull over her revenge. Her new-found knowledge of the true state of affairs has given her an unaccustomed strength. She starts on an ironic note which catches Kenneth off guard but her controlled anger grows into rampant hysteria as Kenneth refuses to confess. Kenneth is slow to catch on that his secret has been revealed. His web of lies and deceit gradually unravels before him. Hilary has obviously decided that she

97

wants Kenneth out of her life and his petulant and childish responses only strengthen her determination. But notice that despite all the provocation and hysteria, Kenneth never actually confesses to his 'crime'. He is evasive and slippery up to the end. As the playwright indicates, you must be careful to orchestrate the emotional crescendo of this scene, observing the pauses and beats as information is revealed and absorbed.

Scenes for Two Women

Amy's View
David Hare

Act 1. The living room of a house in rural Berkshire, not far from Pangbourne. 1979. It is midsummer and past midnight.

Amy Thomas (23) is 'dark-haired, in jeans and a T-shirt, she is . . . thin, with an unmistakable air of quiet resolution'. She works for a London publishing company. Her mother Esme Allen (49) is 'in a simple dress . . . She is surprisingly small, her manner both sensitive and intense. Something in her vulnerability makes people instantly protective of her.' She is a famous West End actress, specialising in boulevard comedies. Her artist-husband, Bernard, died fifteen years previously and she and Evelyn, Bernard's mother, live together in their comfortably faded and slightly bohemian home. Amy has come to visit her mother, bringing her latest boyfriend, Dominic, with her. He is an ambitious film critic and wannabe director. Amy is devoted to Dominic and idealises him. Every evening after work she doggedly distributes Dominic's film magazine. In this scene Esme has just arrived home. One of her little extravagances, and part of her financial naiveté, is to take an hour-long taxi ride all the way back from London after every evening performance. As this scene begins, Dominic has just gone off to repair a bike and the two women are left alone together.

ESME. You'd better say. I'm not such a bad mother.
AMY. What?
ESME. Not such a bad mother that I can't tell. Please, I don't think I can stand an engagement. Do people still do that?
AMY. No. I promise that's not what this is.
ESME. Well?

AMY. It's not serious. I promise you, it's nothing serious at all. I'm waiting to borrow some money.

ESME. Ah, thank goodness. Money, that's all. (*She seems genuinely relieved.*) Of course. How much do you need?

AMY. I'd like five thousand.

ESME. I'm sorry?

AMY. That would be perfect.

ESME. Say that again. (*She suddenly looks at* AMY *directly.*) Why on earth do you want five thousand? There's nothing in the world which costs five thousand pounds.

AMY. If you don't mind, I don't want to say.

ESME. I'm glad, in that case, it's not serious. What would have been serious? Ten?

AMY. I will tell you. I promise I will tell you one day. But you've always said: if I needed anything I was to come to you.

ESME. Why, surely.

AMY. No strings attached. Well, Mother, I'm here.

(ESME *recognizes a note of challenge and rises to it.*)

ESME. That's fine. That's no problem. Now? How do you want it? Do you want a cheque?

AMY. If you could.

ESME. Sure. Yes, of course. Let me do it. Now where exactly did I put my things?

AMY. There. Behind you.

ESME. Of course. (*She takes her bag across to the table.*) How much?

AMY. Five thousand.

ESME. You mean five thousand pounds? Do you mean all in one go? Not in instalments? One day you will give it back?

(AMY *smiles politely at these jokes. Esme has opened her cheque book.*)

AMY. You always said, if ever . . . if ever something came up, you wouldn't ask anything, you'd simply give me whatever I asked.

ESME. Oh yes. (*She pauses a second.*) But first just tell me what this something is.

AMY. Mum . . .

ESME. No, really, I'm joking. I trust you. You know I do. I'm not asking anything. Not a thing. I know if I asked you would tell me, but I'm not going to ask. (*She starts writing.* AMY *just watches.*) Which account is it? I have no idea. There's money from Bernard's estate. Well, something. The ludicrous thing is, I don't make anything at all from the play. I'm losing. By the time I've got a taxi from London, I don't have anything left. (*She looks up at* AMY.) Now what is the date?

AMY. June 25th. It's 1979.

ESME. Well, I know that. Please, do you think I live in a dream? (*She hands* AMY *the cheque.*)

AMY. Thank you.

ESME. How did I do?

AMY. Brilliantly.

ESME. Aren't you proud of your Mum? Cash it quickly before it can bounce. No, really. You're fine. It'll pay. (*She kisses* AMY.) The Trappist. I shan't say any more . . . Well, there it is. It's extraordinary. You've found yourself such a handsome young man.

AMY. Why? Does that surprise you?

ESME. Not in the slightest. Any man's lucky to end up with you.

(*The tone of this is light and friendly but* AMY *is ill at ease.*) The theatre, of course, is full of these people. Good-looking young men who have yet to find out who they are. I see them all the time.

AMY. Is that meant to be Dominic?

ESME. Well, you know him better than me.

(ESME *waits but* AMY *says nothing.*)

But, on the other hand, you have come to ask my opinion . . .

AMY. Have I?

ESME. I think so.

AMY. I'd say on the contrary. Didn't I ask you not to say a word?

ESME. Amy, please, I wasn't born yesterday. When a daughter comes to her mother and says, 'Don't ask anything, I beg you, ask nothing at all . . .', isn't it just a way of saying, 'Quick, Mother, help! I'm desperate to talk'?

(AMY *can't resist smiling at this.*)

AMY. Are you saying I did that unconsciously?

ESME. Unconsciously? Hardly. 'Give me five thousand pounds.' As a way of getting my attention, it would take some beating. Well, wouldn't it?

AMY. Yes. I don't know. Oh perhaps. I'm confused. (*She smiles, relaxing, giving in.*)

ESME. After all that is the basic skill. That *is* my profession. You have to get that right or you might as well give up. You say one thing but you're thinking another. If you can't do that, then truly you shouldn't be doing the job.

(*A look of mischief comes onto* AMY*'s face.*)

AMY. That reminds me, I did see that thing with Deirdre . . .

ESME. Oh, Deirdre!

AMY. I saw that new play which stars Deirdre Keane.

ESME. Well, Deirdre can't even manage the line in the first place, let alone the bit where you think something else.

AMY. She wasn't very good.

ESME. They tell me she's laughable. Apparently she comes on, dressed like a lampshade, a great smear of lipstick right across her face . . .

AMY. They're right . . .

ESME. They say, rolling her eyes like a demented puppy-dog and facing out front all the time. (*She is shaking her head as if outraged.*)

AMY. She got very good reviews.

ESME. Deirdre? She practically goes down on the critics. You've seen her. She's craven. She's always trying to please.

AMY. Is that such a bad thing?

ESME. Of course not. But nobody's explained to her the basis of the whole project.

AMY. Which is?

ESME. Why, to please without seeming to try.

AMY. Oh, I see.

ESME. That's what one's attempting. Of course, we all know it can't be achieved. But that's the ideal. To make it look effortless. (ESME *looks at* AMY *a moment.*) Perhaps it applies just as much in our lives.

(AMY *looks, knowing she cannot avoid things any longer.*)

AMY. Look, Mum, I do know you're desperate to talk to me . . .

ESME. Me?

AMY. There's a thousand questions you're longing to ask . . .

ESME. I can see you're in trouble. In a moment I'm hoping you're going to say why.

AMY. It's not trouble. I wouldn't say trouble exactly . . .

ESME. How's life in your publishing firm?

AMY. Great. They're trying to promote me.

ESME. I'm pleased.

AMY. But one thing's bound up in another.

(AMY *stops dead.* ESME *speaks quietly.*)

ESME. You're expecting a child?

AMY. How did you know? Is it really that obvious?

ESME. It isn't not obvious.

AMY. When did you know?

ESME. The moment I saw you, of course.

(ESME *pushes her uneaten meal aside. She gets up and takes* AMY *in her arms.* AMY *can barely speak through her tears.*)

AMY. Oh God, I'm going to cry . . .

ESME. Well, cry. (*She begins to sob with* AMY.) Please cry, cry all you want to . . .

AMY. No, no, I mustn't . . .

ESME. Oh, Amy . . .

AMY. I mustn't . . . (*She tears herself decisively away.*)

ESME. Why not? It's wonderful . . .

AMY. I mustn't!

ESME. Amy, this is wonderful news.

AMY. Because . . . oh shit, I don't know how to say this. You're going to think I'm insane. (*She is wild, raising her voice.*) I haven't told Dominic. I know this sounds crazy but I don't think I shall.

COMMENTARY: This play focuses on the tortuous relationship between a mother and daughter over an eighteen-year period. Amy and Esme share many characteristics; notice how similar their names are. Amy, like her mother, is quite vulnerable, but she masks it behind a wall of incorruptible moral certainty. There is also something naive and fatally self-destructive about both Amy and Esme (you must read the rest of the play to discover their respective fates). Esme is more of an impulsive hedonist, a skittish, sometimes larger-than-life actress of the old school. Despite her vulnerability, she is tough, caustic and durable. Esme is conscious of her audience even when she is in her own home; for her acting is a way of life. You must create a sense of passionate intensity and tension between the two women. Amy wants Dominic's love and affection, but she tries to win it with her unquestioning devotion and self-sacrifice: 'Amy's View' is that if you give love unconditionally then one day it will be rewarded. Remember that when Esme first sees

Amy she knows intuitively that she is pregnant, the request for money merely confirms her suspicions. Why do you think she wants Amy to confess that she is pregnant and why is Amy so reluctant? Notice how strangely formal her question is; and why does she avoid using the word 'pregnant'? Although the scene deals with serious issues it is important to balance this with a light and when necessary comic touch.

The Beauty Queen of Leenane
Martin McDonagh

Act 1, scene 3. The living-room kitchen of a rural cottage in the west of Ireland . . . It is raining quite heavily.

Mag Folan is 'a stoutish woman in her early seventies with short, tightly permed grey hair and a mouth that gapes slightly . . . Her left hand is somewhat more shrivelled than her right.' She lives with her daughter, Maureen, 'a plain, slim woman of about forty'. At the age of twenty-five, while working as a cleaner, Maureen had a nervous breakdown. Mag's response to this, as she never fails to remind Maureen, was to have her put away in a 'nut-house' for a month. Maureen has lived at home since then, running their small holding and caring for her hypochondriac mother. Mag uses every opportunity to play up her ailments, itemising her 'bad hip' and 'burned hand' and her 'urine infection' (she insists on emptying her 'potty of wee' down the stinking kitchen sink). As the years have passed the two women have become increasingly and dangerously abusive towards each other. Earlier in this scene, Ray Dooley, a lad from the neighbouring farm, stops by to invite them to a going-away do for his uncle, Pato Dooley, but finding that Maureen is out he leaves a note for her which Mag promises to pass on. As the scene begins, just before Maureen returns from feeding the chickens, Mag burns the note.

(*As* RAY*'s footsteps fade,* MAG *gets up, reads the message on the table, goes to the kitchen window and glances out, then finds a box of matches, comes back to the table, strikes a match, lights the message, goes to the range with it burning and drops it inside. Sound of footsteps approaching the front door.* MAG *shuffles back to her rocking chair and sits in it just as* MAUREEN *enters.*)

MAG (*nervously*). Cold, Maureen?

MAUREEN. Of course cold.

MAG. Oh-h.

(MAG *stares at the TV as if engrossed.* MAUREEN *sniffs the air a little, then sits at the table, staring at* MAG.)

MAUREEN. What are you watching?

MAG. I don't know *what* I'm watching. Just waiting for the news I am.

MAUREEN. Oh aye. (*Pause.*) Nobody rang while I was out, I suppose? Ah no.

MAG. Ah no, Maureen. Nobody did ring.

MAUREEN. Ah no.

MAG. No. Who would be ringing?

MAUREEN. No, nobody I suppose. No. (*Pause.*) And nobody visited us either? Ah no.

MAG. Ah no, Maureen. Who would be visiting us?

MAUREEN. Nobody, I suppose. Ah no.

(MAG *glances at* MAUREEN *a second, then back at the TV. Pause.* MAUREEN *gets up, ambles over to the TV, lazily switches it off with the toe of her shoe, ambles back to the kitchen, staring at* MAG *as she passes, turns on the kettle, and leans against the cupboards, looking back in* MAG's *direction.*)

MAG (*nervously*). Em, apart from wee Ray Dooley who passed.

MAUREEN (*knowing*). Oh, did Ray Dooley pass, now?

MAG. He passed, aye, and said hello as he was passing.

MAUREEN. I thought just now you said there was no visitors.

MAG. There was no visitors, no, apart from Ray Dooley who passed.

MAUREEN. Oh, aye, aye, aye. Just to say hello he popped his head in.

MAG. Just to say hello and how is all. Aye. A nice wee lad he is.

MAUREEN. Aye. (*Pause*.) With no news?

MAG. With no news. Sure, what news would a gosawer have?

MAUREEN. None at all, I suppose. Ah, no.

MAG. Ah, no. (*Pause*.) Thinking of getting a car I think he said he was.

MAUREEN. Oh aye?

MAG. A second-hand one.

MAUREEN. Uh-huh?

MAG. To drive, y'know?

MAUREEN. To drive, aye.

MAG. Off Father Welsh – Walsh – Welsh.

MAUREEN. Welsh.

MAG. Welsh.

(MAUREEN *switches off the kettle, pours a sachet of Complan into a mug and fills it up with water*.)

MAUREEN. I'll do you some of your Complan.

MAG. Have I not had me Complan already, Maureen? I have.

MAUREEN. Sure, another one won't hurt.

MAG (*wary*). No, I suppose.

(MAUREEN *tops the drink up with tap water to cool it, stirs it just twice to keep it lumpy, takes the spoon out, hands the drink to* MAG, *then leans back against the table to watch her drink it.* MAG *looks at it in distaste.*)

A bit lumpy, Maureen.

MAUREEN. Never mind lumpy, mam. The lumps will do you good. That's the best part of Complan is the lumps. Drink ahead.

MAG. A little spoon, do you have?

MAUREEN. No, I have no little spoon. There's no little spoons for liars in this house. No little spoons at all. Be drinking ahead.

(MAG *takes the smallest of sickly sips*.)

The whole of it, now!

MAG. I do have a funny tummy, Maureen, and I do have no room.

MAUREEN. Drink ahead, I said! You had room enough to be spouting your lies about Ray Dooley had no message! Did I not meet him on the road beyond as he was going? The lies of you. The whole of that Complan you'll drink now, and suck the lumps down too, and whatever's left you haven't drank, it is over your head I will be emptying it, and you know well enough I mean it!

(MAG *slowly drinks the rest of the sickly brew.*)

Arsing me around, eh? Interfering with my life again? Isn't it enough I've had to be on beck and call for you every day for the past twenty year? Is it one evening out you begrudge me?

MAG. Young girls should not be out gallivanting with fellas . . . !

MAUREEN. Young girls! I'm forty years old, for feck's sake! Finish it!

(MAG *drinks again.*)

'Young girls'! That's the best yet. And how did Annette or Margo ever get married if it wasn't first out gallivanting that they were?

MAG. I didn't know.

MAUREEN. Drink!

MAG. I don't like it, Maureen.

MAUREEN. Would you like it better over your head?

(MAG *drinks again.*)

I'll tell you, eh? 'Young girls out gallivanting.' I've heard it all now. What have I ever done but *kissed* two men the past forty year?

MAG. Two men is plenty!

MAUREEN. Finish!

MAG. I've finished!

(MAG *holds out the mug.* MAUREEN *washes it.*)

Two men is two men too much!

MAUREEN. To you, maybe. To you. Not to me.

MAG. Two men too much!

MAUREEN. Do you think I like being stuck up here with you? Eh? Like a dried up oul . . .

MAG. Whore!

(MAUREEN *laughs*.)

MAUREEN. 'Whore'? (*Pause*.) Do I not *wish*, now? Do I not wish? (*Pause*.) Sometimes I *dream* . . .

MAG. Of being a . . . ?

MAUREEN. Of anything! (*Pause. Quietly*.) Of anything. Other than this.

MAG. Well an odd dream that is!

MAUREEN. It's not at all. Not at all is it an odd dream. (*Pause*.) And if it is it's not the only odd dream I do have. Do you want to be hearing another one?

MAG. I don't.

MAUREEN. I have a dream sometimes there of you, dressed all nice and white, in your coffin there, and me all in black looking in on you, and a fella beside me there, comforting me, the smell of aftershave off him, his arm round me waist. And the fella asks me then if I'll be going for a drink with him at his place after.

MAG. And what do you say?

MAUREEN. I say 'Aye, what's stopping me now?'

MAG. You don't!

MAUREEN. I do!

MAG. At me funeral?

MAUREEN. At your bloody wake, sure! Is even sooner!

MAG. Well that's not a nice thing to be dreaming!

MAUREEN. I know it's not, sure, and it isn't a *dream*-dream at all. It's more of a day-dream. Y'know, something happy to be thinking of when I'm scraping the skitter out of them hens.

MAG. Not at all is that a nice dream. That's a mean dream.

MAUREEN. I don't know if it is or it isn't.

(*Pause.* MAUREEN *sits at the table with a pack of Kimberley biscuits.*)

I suppose now you'll never be dying. You'll be hanging on for ever, just to spite me.

MAG. I *will* be hanging on for ever!

MAUREEN. I know well you will!

MAG. Seventy you'll be at my wake, and then how many men'll there be round your waist with their aftershave?

MAUREEN. None at all, I suppose.

MAG. None at all is right!

MAUREEN. Oh aye. (*Pause.*) Do you want a Kimberley?

MAG (*pause*). Have we no shortbread fingers?

MAUREEN. No, you've ate all the shortbread fingers. Like a pig.

MAG. I'll have a Kimberley so, although I don't like Kimberleys. I don't know why you get Kimberleys at all. Kimberleys are horrible.

MAUREEN. Me world doesn't revolve around your taste in biscuits.

(MAUREEN *gives* MAG *a biscuit.* MAG *eats.*)

MAG (*pause*). You'll be going to this do tomorrow so?

MAUREEN. I will. (*Pause.*) It'll be good to see Pato again anyways. I didn't even know he was home.

MAG. But it's all them oul Yanks'll be there tomorrow.

MAUREEN. So?

MAG. You said you couldn't stand the Yanks yesterday. The crux of the matter yesterday you said it was.

MAUREEN. Well, I suppose now, mother, I will have to be changing me mind, but, sure, isn't that a woman's prerogative?

MAG (*quietly*). It's only prerogatives when it suits you.

MAUREEN. Don't go using big words you don't understand, now, mam.

MAG (*sneers. Pause*). This invitation was open to me too, if you'd like to know.

MAUREEN (*half-laughing*). Do you think you'll be coming?

MAG. I won't, I suppose.

MAUREEN. You suppose right enough. Lying the head off you, like the babby of a tinker.

MAG. I was only saying.

MAUREEN. Well, don't be saying. (*Pause.*) I think we might take a drive into Westport later, if it doesn't rain.

MAG (*brighter*). Will we take a drive?

MAUREEN. We could take a little drive for ourselves.

MAG. We could now. It's a while since we did take a nice drive. We could get some shortbread fingers.

MAUREEN. Later on, I'm saying.

MAG. Later on. Not just now.

MAUREEN. Not just now. Sure, you've only just had your Complan now.

(MAG *gives her a dirty look. Pause.*)

Aye, Westport. Aye. And I think I might pick up a nice little dress for meself while I'm here. For the do tomorrow, y'know?

(MAUREEN *looks across at* MAG, *who looks back at her, irritated. Blackout.*)

COMMENTARY: McDonagh portrays an isolated rural district where cruelty and malice are commonplace. Despite the isolation, this is a tightly-knit community where 'everybody know everybody else's business'. Everyone thrives on gossip. For Mag and Maureen the harsh poverty of their home has an inexorably tragic influence over their lives. They co-exist in a constant state of hate, resentment and bitterness. In their claustrophobic cottage they have become worst enemies. There is no glimmer of love or affection in their relationship; instead they wage an unrelenting battle for one-upmanship in the humdrum routines of their daily lives. Maureen meets Mag's cantankerous and wheedling ways with her own vindictive spite. Their only enjoyment comes from the perverse delight of tormenting and outwitting each other. The days are filled with the endless rituals of eating and drinking often unpalatable food and drink. It is important to stress the delight that Mag and Maureen take in baiting one another. There is a wild and blackly comic side to this relationship that requires deft and skilful playing.

(NB The following scene from this play can be found on page 3 of this volume.)

The Cripple of Inishmaan
Martin McDonagh

Act 1, scene 1. A small country shop on the remote island of Inishmaan off the west coast of Ireland. 1934.

Eileen Osbourne (mid 60s) and her sister Kate (mid 60s) own the village shop. For the past fifteen years they have been 'Aunties' to the orphaned Billy Claven; they are not his real aunts but took him in and cared for him when his own parents died in mysterious circumstances. They have a reputation in the village for being 'funny' because of their sometimes rather eccentric behaviour. This scene opens the play with Eileen 'placing some more cans onto the shelves' as Kate enters from the back room.

KATE. Is Billy not yet home?

EILEEN. Not yet is Billy home.

KATE. I do worry awful about Billy when he's late returning home.

EILEEN. I banged me arm on a can of peas worrying about Cripple Billy.

KATE. Was it your bad arm?

EILEEN. No, it was me other arm.

KATE. It would have been worse if you'd banged your bad arm.

EILEEN. It would have been worse, although it still hurt.

KATE. Now you have two bad arms.

EILEEN. Well, I have one bad arm and one arm with a knock.

KATE. The knock will go away.

EILEEN. The knock will go away.

KATE. And you'll be left with the one bad arm.

EILEEN. The one bad arm will never go away.

KATE. Until the day you die.

EILEEN. I should think about poor Billy, who has not only bad arms but bad legs too.

KATE. Billy has a host of troubles.

EILEEN. Billy has a hundred troubles.

KATE. What time was this his appointment with McSharry was and his chest?

EILEEN. I don't know what time.

KATE. I do worry awful about Billy when he's late in returning, d'you know?

EILEEN. Already once you've said that sentence.

KATE. Am I not allowed to repeat me sentences so when I'm worried.

EILEEN. You *are* allowed.

KATE (*pause*). Billy may've fell down a hole with them feet of his.

EILEEN. Billy has sense enough not to fall down holes, sure. That's more like something Bartley McCormick'd do is fall down holes.

KATE. Do you remember the time Bartley McCormick fell down the hole?

EILEEN. Bartley McCormick's an awful thick.

KATE. He's either a thick or he doesn't look where he's going proper. (*Pause.*) Has the egg-man been?

EILEEN. He has but he had no eggs.

KATE. A waste of time him coming, so.

EILEEN. Well it was nice of him to come and not have us waiting for eggs that would never arrive.

KATE. If only Billy would pay us the same courtesy. Not with eggs but to come home quick and not have us worrying.

EILEEN. Maybe Billy stopped to look at a cow like the other time.

117

KATE. A fool waste of time that is, looking at cows.

EILEEN. If it makes him happy, sure, what harm? There are a hundred worse things to occupy a lad's time than cow-watching. Things would land him up in hell. Not just late for his tea.

KATE. Kissing lasses.

EILEEN. Kissing lasses.

KATE (*pause*). Ah, no chance of that with poor Billy.

EILEEN. Poor Billy'll never be getting kissed. Unless it was be a blind girl.

KATE. A blind girl or a backward girl.

EILEEN. Or Jim Finnegan's daughter.

KATE. She'd kiss anything.

EILEEN. She'd kiss a bald donkey.

KATE. She'd kiss a bald donkey. And she'd still probably draw the line at Billy. Poor Billy.

EILEEN. A shame too.

KATE. A shame too, because Billy does have a sweet face if you ignore the rest of him.

EILEEN. Well he doesn't really.

KATE. He has a bit of a sweet face.

EILEEN. Well he doesn't really, Kate.

KATE. Or his *eyes*, I'm saying. They're nice enough.

EILEEN. Not being cruel to Billy but you'd see nicer eyes on a goat. If he had a nice personality you'd say all well and good, but all Billy has is he goes around staring at cows.

KATE. I'd like to ask him one day what good he gets, staring at cows.

EILEEN. Staring at cows and reading books then.

KATE. No one'll ever marry him. We'll be stuck with him 'til the day we die.

EILEEN. We will. (*Pause.*) I don't mind being stuck with him.

KATE. *I* don't mind being stuck with him. Billy's a good gosawer, despiting the cows.

EILEEN. I hope that the news from McSharry was nothing to worry o'er.

KATE. I hope he gets home soon and not have us worrying. I do worry awful when Billy's late in returning.

COMMENTARY: This play presents a picture of a rural backwater where the news of a goose biting a cat's tail is a major event. The sisters' store is a centre of gossip for the villagers. It is important to create a sense of the physical layout of the store as the two women continue working as they chatter away. Notice that they each have a distinct idiom and rhythm to the way they speak, and yet they also have an easy badinage and shorthand way of speaking to each other. They repeat and echo each other's and their own lines, and the timing of these lines is crucial to gain maximum comic impact. There is something a little childlike about Kate in contrast to her more icy sister. Despite their apparently disparaging and cruel remarks about Billy it is important to convey just how much his two 'Aunties' adore him. It is somewhat ironic that they should cast judgement on Billy's romantic chances when their own spinsterish lives have been quite isolated and barren.

Kindertransport
Diane Samuels

Act 2, scene 1. The spare storage room in Evelyn's house in an outer London suburb in recent times.

Faith (early 20s) is Evelyn's daughter and Lil Miller's (80s) granddaughter. During the Second World War Evelyn was sent to England from Nazi Germany by her Jewish parents and she was eventually adopted by Lil. Faith is completely unaware of her mother's true past. She is a student and lives at home with her divorced mother, but she is in the process of getting a flat of her own. Evelyn and Faith have come up to the attic to see if there is anything suitable for Faith to take to her new flat. But as they start going through the boxes Faith gets cold feet and decides, much to her mother's annoyance, to stay at home after all. Evelyn storms off and vents her frustration in a manic bout of house cleaning. Faith stays in the attic going through the meticulously packed boxes of her old toys, creating a terrible mess. Lil, who is visiting her daughter and granddaughter, suggests that Faith should tidy up as a goodwill gesture towards her mother. As this scene starts Lil has just returned to the attic with a tray of tea for them to share.

FAITH. I don't want any tea.

LIL. Don't make me have it on my own.

FAITH. What about Mum?

LIL. She's polishing furniture.

FAITH. Has she had the vacuum out yet?

LIL. Stop it.

FAITH. I'm sorry. I'm not hungry.

LIL (*signalling at the mess*). Get on with it, Faith.

FAITH. Gran . . .

LIL. Now.

FAITH. If you don't mind, I'm just looking . . .

LIL (*bending down to pick things up*). Time to come out and face the music, Princess Hideaway.

FAITH. Don't call me that.

LIL. Don't do it then.

FAITH. Look what I've found . . .

(FAITH *pulls out the 'Rattenfänger' book*.)

LIL. Stop poking about, will you.

FAITH. It's the Ratcatcher story. I didn't know we had a copy.

LIL. What Ratcatcher story?

FAITH. You know, 'The Ratcatcher ever-ready in the shadows'.

LIL. Don't recall it.

FAITH. Yes you do. All the parents say, 'If you're not good the Ratcatcher will come and get you.' But the children don't listen. And he comes out of the dark night with his spiky nails and razor eyes and tempts them with sweets. And they're so naughty that they follow him into the abyss.

LIL. Why d'you think I know it?

FAITH. Mum used to tell me. She said she was told it when she was little.

LIL. She must have read it herself.

FAITH. She can't have done. Not from this book. It's in German.

LIL. Let me see.

(LIL *takes the book and opens it*.)

LIL. Where did you get this?

FAITH. That box.

(LIL *looks in the box at the letters and photos*.)

FAITH. Did it belong to the little Jewish girl you had staying with you during the war?

LIL. What d'you mean?

121

(FAITH *picks up a photo and shows it to* LIL.)

FAITH. Eva something.

LIL. How d'you know about this Eva?

FAITH. I read some stuff.

LIL. What have you read?

FAITH. Letters from her parents, bits from her diary . . .

LIL. You should leave things alone.

FAITH. D'you know why Mum's got all her belongings?

LIL. No idea.

FAITH. I'm surprised you've never mentioned her.

LIL. A million things happened during the war.

FAITH. Were you close?

LIL. She wasn't with us for long.

FAITH. It must have been for at least two years . . .

LIL. Was it?

FAITH. Why are you being so cagey?

LIL. I'm hungry for my tea.

FAITH (*joking*). Did you kill her and try to hide the evidence?

LIL. Don't be so bloody stupid!

FAITH. Gran?

LIL. I didn't think that your mother had kept anything from that time.

FAITH. It's upset you, hasn't it?

LIL. I don't know why.

FAITH. Did something bad happen to her?

LIL. To who?

FAITH (*holding up the photo*). Little Eva.

LIL. No. No. She's alright.

FAITH. D'you know where she is?

LIL. Stop going on at me will you.

FAITH. It's OK. Sorry. Don't worry. I'll ask Mum.

LIL. No. Don't. Don't you dare.

FAITH. Why not?

LIL. Just leave it.

FAITH. Why?

(LIL *is silent*.)

FAITH. What?

LIL. Give me that photo.

FAITH. Why should I?

LIL. These are your mother's private possessions, Faith.

(FAITH *pulls back and looks at the photo closely*.)

(LIL *holds out her hand for it*.)

(FAITH *keeps hold*.)

FAITH. No they're not. They really belong to that Eva . . .

(LIL *keeps holding out her hand*.)

LIL. Your mother's things.

FAITH. Who is this little girl?

LIL. Faith.

FAITH. Who?

(LIL *looks down*.)

FAITH. Is she something to do with Mum?

LIL. Faith.

FAITH. Is she?

LIL. You shouldn't have looked at them.

FAITH. Is she Mum?

LIL. Put them away now.

FAITH. Shit.

LIL. Put them away.

FAITH. You told me she was three days old when she came to you.

LIL. What am I meant to say?

FAITH. Just answer.

LIL. She was nine years when she came.

FAITH. And she was called Eva?

LIL. I'm not going to lie.

FAITH. And she spoke German and wore a yellow star?

LIL. There was no yellow star.

FAITH. But she was Jewish?

LIL. It was a long time ago.

FAITH. This is unbelievable.

LIL. You really shouldn't have looked.

FAITH. I've asked you both so many times about her real family.

LIL. Aren't I real now?

FAITH. Did you ever meet her parents?

LIL. No.

FAITH. Do you know what happened to them?

LIL. They died.

FAITH. Why make a secret out of it?

LIL. She just wanted to put the past behind her. It was for the best.

FAITH. Whose best?

LIL. Hers.

FAITH. What about mine?

LIL. Don't be so bloody selfish.

FAITH. Don't you think that this affects me?

LIL. It affects her more.

FAITH. I know nothing about her.

LIL. She's still your mam, Faith. Don't make a big deal out of something that was over and done with before you were born.

FAITH. What was the point in having me if she was going to cut herself off?

COMMENTARY: Between 1938 and the outbreak of war more than 10,000 mostly Jewish children were shipped out by their parents on the Kindertransport from Nazi Germany to Britain. Nine-year-old Eva was sent on the Kindertransport and ended up in Manchester with Lil Miller. Gradually Eva assimilated to life in Britain, totally denying her roots and background, changing her name to Evelyn and converting from Judaism to Christianity. Over the years all of this has been completely hidden from Faith by both her mother and grandmother. The tension in this scene must grow between the two women. As Faith begins to unravel her mother's past she increasingly puts Lil on the spot. At first Lil is not aware of just what it is that Faith has uncovered, her sole concern is to get the place tidied up. It is only when the 'Rattenfänger' book appears that she realises just what it is that Faith is discovering, and notice how her mood changes as a result. Faith is in the process of discovering not only her mother's past but by association her own as well. Faith desperately wants to know who she is and who her mother is and was. The toys, books, letters and photos are her clues. Each of these is an important prop; a tangible memento of the past for Lil and a clue for Faith. She is angry at what she sees is the double conspiracy of secrecy and lies perpetrated by both Lil and Evelyn: it is the denial of her roots and her history. Lil tries to take on the role of mediator. She is reluctant to betray Evelyn's secret and she realises that it has now become her secret too. Lil actively encouraged and supported the transformation of German-Jewish Eva into English-Christian Evelyn, believing that this was the only way of helping her to deal with her tragic situation. Until this moment in the play when Faith opens Eva/Evelyn's box the secret has been completely suppressed for over forty years. Why do you think Lil finally gives in and reveals the truth to Faith?

Low Level Panic
Clare McIntyre

Scene 5. A bathroom in a shared flat.

Mary (20s) works in an office. Late one evening, after leaving work on her bicycle, she was brutally sexually assaulted by two young thugs. This has had a traumatic effect on her and she cannot stop thinking over the senseless events of that night. Jo (20s) is Mary's room-mate. She is slightly plump and obsessed with her weight, her looks and her vivid sexual fantasies. As this scene opens the two girls are getting ready to go out to a party and Mary is swigging wine from a bottle. Both girls are dressed in their 'party gear'.

JO (*coming in*). If you don't come to this party I'll kill you.
MARY. It was because I was dressed up.
JO. We've been over this before Mary: you weren't dressed up.
MARY. I was more dressed up than usual.
JO. You were wearing a skirt.
MARY. For me I was dressed up.
JO. You weren't dressed up at all. You never dress up. And what if you were?
MARY. I remember being all dolled up.
JO. I can't remember ever seeing you all dolled up.
MARY. I am now.
JO. Apart from now I don't.
MARY. I was wearing those enamel bracelets I've got. I can't remember why . . . but I was looking nice. I know I was. I just felt it. Sometimes you do feel that don't you? Sometimes you just know you're looking okay. It's not like

I was looking like anything in particular. I just felt nice. That's more it. I'd felt nice when I'd been cycling to work: all cool and breezy. I don't remember what I looked like but I remember how I felt.

JO. But you weren't dressed up.

MARY. I wasn't concentrating.

JO. You weren't.

MARY. No.

JO. You always wore a skirt didn't you?

MARY. Had to.

JO. You were just dressed ordinary.

MARY. They didn't think so.

JO. Boys like that don't think, not with their brains that is. They might think a bit with their dicks but not with their brains they don't. Not at all. They don't even know where their brains are.

MARY. I'm sure I was looking nice . . . for me, that is.

JO. You are nice looking.

MARY. I must have been looking sexy but I didn't know it. They must have thought I was looking all dressed up and sexy.

JO. What's wrong with looking sexy?

MARY. I want to look like I feel.

JO. You do. You must do. You just look natural.

MARY. Not in a bloody party dress I don't. Not all done up in a party dress. It makes me feel like I did then, all flimsy and open and . . .

JO. And women love it.

MARY. What?

JO. Being sexy.

MARY. Do they?

JO. 'Course they do.

MARY. And what's being sexy?

JO. Oh come on.

MARY. Feeling like this?

JO. Yes. What's wrong with that?

MARY. It feels horrible.

JO. Why can't you enjoy it?

MARY. Because . . .

JO. You won't let yourself will you? Just relax.

MARY. I'm trying.

JO. You've got to feel good about yourself or nothing'll happen.

MARY. Nothing like what?

JO. I'm going to count to ten and then I'm going to *scream*.

MARY. So this looks sexy does it? (*Holding her dress up against her.*)

JO. 'Course it does . . . No, it doesn't. It doesn't look sexy at all. Okay?

MARY. No. I feel like someone else. I feel funny and peculiar and a million miles from confident and that's fine and terrific and just as it should be and I'm to go out and enjoy myself. Right?

JO. Yes.

MARY. That's what you want me to do?

JO. Yes. 'Cos you will. You're just nervous. I'm nervous for Heaven's sake.

MARY. Are you?

JO. Yes. No.

MARY. Which?

JO. I don't know.

MARY. But what . . .

JO. Stop asking questions. You'll disappear up your own bum.

MARY. I think I'm in a coma.

JO. Well rally round or we'll be late.

MARY. 'Pornography's the tip of the iceberg.' Somebody said that.

JO. Oh my God. Cut my wrists. Cut my wrists.

128

MARY. They were right.

JO. And we've all got to learn to live with it.

MARY. I can't . . .

JO. In the course of a day, a day without too much effort put into it you'll see more pictures of naked breasts than you will naked bollocks. Breast for breast, bollock for bollock, breasts will come out on top.

MARY. Is that . . . ?

JO. Try and stop thinking for once will you? For five minutes, however long it's going to take you to get yourself out of this house and on to the street. (*She goes out.*)

MARY (*has to shout to be heard*). What matters then? Things do matter, you know. We've got to understand why we think whatever it is we do think otherwise how are we meant to live with ourselves? I mean that's what we are. We are what we think about things.

(JO *enters carrying her coat – ready, apart from final touches of make-up, to leave.*)

Most of the time you know what you think. You know if you like oranges or not or what you feel like having for tea. But none of that matters. And you can't say that everything that does matter somehow has got nothing to do with you 'cos it has got something to do with you whether you like it or not. It has. 'Cos we're all alive and we all walk down the street and see things and you can't pretend those things don't get inside your head somehow because they do. Even if you're not aware of it they do. So they're there for you to make sense of. You've got to decide what you feel about them and you can't just say you feel whatever it is you do just because that's the way you do because that isn't true. You're not born thinking the way you think. Things happen which make you think like that. You're making decisions all the time even if what you're deciding to do is not to think about something. That's a decision. I mean there are some people who don't

129

think they think at all, who think they're just thick, but they are thinking because all that stuff they see is getting into their heads just like it's getting into mine. It's part of them like it's part of you and me. It's there for them to think about. It's hopeless to say you don't have to think about things because you do. You've got to.

JO. You're pissed aren't you?

MARY. Yup.

JO. Aren't you?

MARY. Yup.

JO. Coming?

MARY. Yup.

JO. Bloody liability.

MARY. Yup.

COMMENTARY: This play vividly and often comically confronts how a brutal act of male violence affects one woman and her two flatmates. The author gives no personal details about the characters so you might want to create your own histories for them. The personalities of Jo and Mary are quite different and you must show how their attitudes in this scene reflect this. Jo has been trying desperately to get Mary out of the depression that seems to be on the verge of overwhelming her. As Mary struggles to come to terms with what has happened to her, Jo jollies her along saying, 'You need to get yourself out of yourself, forget who you are and have a good time.' But their very preparations for the party exacerbate Mary's anxieties. She starts fretting that it was the way she was dressed on that fateful evening that played such an important part in leading the boys on. More than anything Jo just wants to get to the party. Notice that there is a humour in the girls' camaraderie but use it carefully to counter the underlying horror of Mary's victimisation. Since the scene, and the play as a whole, deal with men's sexual perceptions of women, you will want to be cautious in how you portray the physical and sexual aspects of Mary and Jo.

The Memory of Water
Shelagh Stevenson

Scene 1. A bedroom, dominated by a double bed. The room is slightly old-fashioned. There is a pile of books on the bedside table. Morning.

Mary (39) is a successful and busy consultant neurologist at a London hospital. She is single and for the past five years has been having an affair with a married man. Teresa (early 40s) is Mary's elder sister. She is married to Frank and together they run a business selling 'health supplements'. Following the recent death of their mother, Vi, they have come back to her house to prepare for the funeral. Their younger sister, Catherine, will also be joining them. As the scene begins Mary is lying in her mother's bed wearing Ray-Ban sunglasses.

(MARY *is lying prostrate. She stirs and gets out of bed, goes to the dressing-table, opens drawers, rifles through them. The phone rings.*)

MARY. Hello? . . . What time is it? . . . I wouldn't be talking to you if I was, would I? I'd be unconscious . . . Where are you? . . . Jesus . . . you're what? So will you want me to pick you up from the station?

(*The door opens and* TERESA *comes in.*)

TERESA. Oh . . .

MARY. Hold on . . . (*To* TERESA.) It's not for you.

TERESA. Who is it?

MARY (*to caller*). What? She's gone where? . . . OK, OK. I'll see you later. Are you sure you don't want me to pick you up –

(*She's cut off.*)

Hello? . . . Shit.

TERESA. Who was that?

MARY. A nuisance caller. We struck up a rapport.

TERESA. He's not staying here, is he?

MARY. Who?

TERESA. I'm presuming it's your boyfriend.

MARY. How much sleep have I had?

(*She picks up a portable alarm clock and peers at it.*)

TERESA. How's his wife?

MARY. Jesus. Two and a half hours.

(*She flops back on the pillows. Looks at* TERESA.)

Why are you looking so awake?

TERESA. I've been up since quarter past five. Presumably he's leaving her at home, then.

MARY. You've got that slight edge in your voice. Like a blunt saw.

TERESA. I'm just asking –

MARY. Of course he's bloody leaving her at home. She's gone to stay with her mother.

TERESA. I thought she was ill.

MARY. Maybe she went in an iron lung. Maybe she made a miracle recovery. I don't know. I didn't ask.

TERESA. Where's he going to sleep?

MARY. What?

TERESA. You can't sleep with him in that bed.

MARY. He's staying in an hotel.

TERESA. I thought it might be something important.

MARY. What?

TERESA. The phone. Funeral directors or something.

MARY. We've done all that. Can I go back to sleep?

TERESA. And where's Catherine?

MARY. She said she might stay over with someone.

TERESA. Does she still have friends here?

MARY. Probably. I don't know.

(*She turns away, settles down, and shuts her eyes.* TERESA *watches her for a while.*)

TERESA. She could have phoned to say. Anything could have happened to her. It's still snowing.

MARY. She's thirty-three, Teresa.

TERESA. The roads are terrible.

MARY. She'll get a taxi.

TERESA. Probably just as well she didn't come home. She'd have probably drunk four bottles of cider and been brought home in a police car. And then she'd have been sick all over the television.

MARY. She was thirteen when she did that.

TERESA. She was lucky she didn't get electrocuted.

MARY. It wasn't switched on.

TERESA. Yes it was, I was watching it. It was *The High Chaparral*.

MARY. No it wasn't. I wish you'd stop remembering things that didn't actually happen.

TERESA. I was there. You weren't.

(MARY *gives up trying to sleep. Sits up.*)

MARY. I was there.

TERESA. That was the other time. The time when she ate the cannabis.

MARY. That was me. I ate hash cookies.

TERESA. It was Catherine.

MARY. It was me.

TERESA. I was there.

MARY. So where was I?

TERESA. Doing your homework probably. Dissecting frogs. Skinning live rabbits. Strangling cats. The usual.

MARY. Teresa. I'd like to get another hour's sleep. I'm not in the mood, OK?

(*She tries to settle down in the bed, and pulls something out that's causing her discomfort: a glass contraption with a rubber bulb at one end. She puts it on the bedside table and settles down again.* TERESA *picks it up.*)

TERESA. Oh, for God's sake . . . Is this what I think it is?

MARY. I don't know. What d'you think it is?

TERESA. A breast pump.

MARY. I found it on top of the wardrobe. I think I'd like to have it.

TERESA. Why?

MARY. Because you've got the watch and the engagement ring.

TERESA. For Lucy. Not for me. For Lucy.

MARY. OK. So you want the breast pump. Have it.

TERESA. I don't want it.

MARY. Good. That's settled. Now let me go to sleep.

TERESA. You can't just take things willy-nilly.

MARY. You did.

TERESA. Oh, I see. I see what this is about.

(MARY *sits up.*)

MARY. It's not about anything, it's about me trying to get some sleep. For Christ's sake, Teresa, it's too early in the morning for this.

(MARY *pulls the covers over her head. Silence.* TERESA *goes to the door, turns back.*)

TERESA. Could you keep off the phone, I'm waiting for Frank to ring and my mobile's recharging –

MARY. If you take that phone to the funeral this time –

TERESA. Oh, go to sleep.

(MARY *sits up.*)

MARY. I'm surprised Dad didn't burst out of his coffin and punch you.

TERESA. I didn't know it was in my bag.

MARY. You could have turned it off. You didn't have to speak to them.

TERESA. I didn't speak to them.

MARY. You did. I heard you. You told them you were in a meeting.

TERESA. You're imagining this. This is a completely false memory.

MARY. All memories are false.

TERESA. Mine aren't.

MARY. Yours in particular.

TERESA. Oh, I see, mine are all false but yours aren't.

MARY. That's not what I said.

TERESA. And what's with the Ray-Bans?

(MARY *takes them off*.)

MARY. I couldn't sleep with the light on.

TERESA. You could have turned it off.

MARY. I was frightened of the dark.

TERESA. When did this start?

MARY. It's all right for you. You're not sleeping in her bed.

TERESA. Oh, for goodness' sake.

MARY. You grabbed the spare room pretty sharpish.

TERESA. I was here first.

MARY. Have the sheets been changed?

TERESA. Yes.

MARY. When?

TERESA. What difference does it make?

MARY. I don't like sleeping in her bed, that's all.

TERESA. She didn't die in it.

MARY. She was the last person in it. It's full of bits of skin and hair that belong to her –

TERESA. Stop it –

MARY. And it makes me feel uncomfortable –

TERESA. What, bits of skin and hair?

MARY. You shed cells. They fall off when you're asleep. I found a toenail before.

TERESA. Please.

MARY. I thought I might keep it in a locket round my neck. Or maybe you'd like it –

TERESA. Stop it, for goodness' sake.

(TERESA *picks up a book from the bedside table.*)

You can't leave work alone for five minutes, can you, even at a time like this?

MARY. I've a very sick patient.

TERESA. You had a very sick mother.

MARY. Don't start, Teresa.

TERESA. Oh, she never complained. Because your job's important. I mean, doctors are second to God, whereas Frank and I only have a business to run, so obviously we could drop everything at a moment's notice.

MARY. It's not my fault.

(*Silence.*)

TERESA. Why do we always do this?

MARY. What?

TERESA. Why do we always argue?

MARY. We don't argue, we bicker.

TERESA. OK, why do we bicker?

MARY. Because we don't get on.

TERESA. Yes we do.

MARY. Oh, have it your own way.

(*She unscrews the whiskey and takes a swig.* TERESA *looks at her, aghast.*)

TERESA. You haven't even got out of bed yet.

MARY. It's the only way we're going to get through this.

(*She offers it to* TERESA *who shakes her head.*)

TERESA. D'you often have a drink in the morning?

MARY. Of course I bloody don't, what d'you think I am?

TERESA. Lots of doctors are alcoholics. It's the stress.

MARY. Someone dies, you drink whiskey. It's normal, it's a sedative, it's what normal people do at abnormal times.

(*She takes another swig. Silence.*)

OK. Let's be nice to each other.

(*Silence.*)

What do people usually talk about when their mother's just died?

TERESA. I don't know. Funeral arrangements. What colour coffin. I've got a list somewhere.

MARY. There should be a set form. Like those books on wedding etiquette. Sudden Death Etiquette. Lesson One. Breaking the news. Phrases to avoid include: guess what?

TERESA. I was distraught, I wasn't thinking properly –

MARY. I thought you'd won the lottery or something –

TERESA. It's quite tricky for you, being nice, isn't it?

MARY. Sorry. I forgot. How are you feeling?

(*TERESA looks at her watch.*)

TERESA. I was expecting him to phone an hour ago.

MARY. I'm not talking about Frank.

TERESA. I don't know how I feel. Everything I eat tastes of salt.

(*Silence. TERESA crosses the room and takes the whiskey from MARY. She takes a swig and grimaces.*)

TERESA. Salt. Everything tastes of it.

COMMENTARY: This is a drama which reveals and revels in the patterns and strains of family life. From the moment this scene starts the bickering (not arguing, as they say) begins. Although they are both grown-ups, the sibling rivalries and jealousies of their childhood are all too apparent. They are thrown together merely because they are related. Notice that within this potentially tragic framework the writer has created a vivacious comedy. They cannot help irritating and annoying each other; everything they say is an invitation for squabbling contradictions. As the play progresses, the self-absorbed and unhappy sisters rake over their dysfunctional lives and memories. Each of them has tried to cut themselves off from their mother, and all three, in different ways, have failed. In this scene how much do you think they are affected by being in their mother's bedroom?

My Mother Said I Never Should
Charlotte Keatley

Act 1, scene 6. A council flat in Mosside, Manchester, early December 1971.

Jackie (19½) is doing a degree course at art school in Manchester. She became pregnant and had a baby, Rosie. The father of the baby is married with children. He and Jackie agreed to lead separate lives. Margaret (40) is Jackie's mother. When Rosie is three months old Jackie finds it all just too much and phones her mother in despair and begs her to take Rosie away. Margaret agrees on the condition that she is allowed to raise Rosie as if she were her own daughter. In her desperation Jackie agrees to this condition. As the scene opens, Jackie is packing baby clothes into a holdall.

RADIO (*Manchester DJ*). . . . Today's highest temperature is expected to be a cold 3°, so wrap up warm. Most roads in the city have been cleared now, but there's still ice and snow on the Pennines, and the forecast is more snow tonight. Police are asking motorists leaving Manchester on Northbound routes to drive slowly because of black ice. Meanwhile, here's something to remind you of summer days . . . (*'Honky Tonk Woman'*.)

JACKIE (*packing hurriedly*). I wanted it to look nice and now it won't all go in!

(ROSIE *yells*.)

JACKIE (*hits transistor, which goes off*). Ssh, Rosie, please –

(ROSIE *yells*.)

JACKIE. Shut up!

(ROSIE *stops crying abruptly*.)

138

JACKIE (*gently*). Ssh, ssh, there now . . . Where do you get the energy from, yelling all night? (*Bends over Moses basket, sings haphazard tune.*) My little rabbit, in your little basket . . .

(ROSIE *coos.*)

JACKIE. Sleep, beautiful . . . ssh . . .

(ROSIE *makes a little cry as* JACKIE *moves away to pack again.*)

JACKIE (*bends over* ROSIE *again*). Please don't be crying when Mummy and Daddy arrive! – Where's your red sock? (*Picks it up and dangles it over* ROSIE, *who quietens during:*) Look, it fell out! Give me a smile – yes! There. I even washed your red sock. Washed everything, don't want Mummy to think – (*Holding back tears.*) I've got to clear up, Rosie. – All these ashtrays, Sandra and Hugh last night, they never think about you, do they? (*Picks up ashtray.*)

MARGARET (*from off*). Hello?

JACKIE. Oh shit, the mess – Come in!

MARGARET (*entering*). Hello Jackie.

JACKIE (*immediately casual*). Hi Mummy.

MARGARET. It's not locked!

JACKIE. I knew it would be you.

MARGARET. You've been smoking.

JACKIE. Journey from London OK?

MARGARET. Not how I remembered, Mosside. All these tower blocks . . .

JACKIE. Is Daddy – he's not –

MARGARET. Waiting in the car.

JACKIE. He didn't mind? – I'm sorry, I couldn't face –

MARGARET. He understands.

(*Pause.*)

JACKIE. This is Rosie, Mummy.

MARGARET. I – came up the stairs. (*Pause.*) Lift is out of order. (*Pause.*) Lot of stairs.

JACKIE. . . . Please.

MARGARET (*long pause*). Three months.

JACKIE. Say hello.

MARGARET (*goes to the Moses basket. Pause*). Pretty.

JACKIE (*goes also*). You think so?

MARGARET. You had curly eyelashes like that.

JACKIE (*pleased*). Did I?

MARGARET. Hello Rosie . . . (*Kisses her.*)

JACKIE. Don't wake her!

MARGARET. Of course not!

JACKIE. I'm sorry, it's just –

MARGARET. You think I don't know?

(ROSIE *coos quietly.*)

MARGARET (*very tenderly*). Ssh, there now.

(ROSIE *murmurs.*)

JACKIE (*turns away*). I've packed her things . . . here.
(*Gives* MARGARET *the holdall.*) And her bottles are in
this carrier. There's a bit of powdered milk left –

MARGARET. Oh you really don't need –

JACKIE. Well what would I do with it?

(*Awkward pause.* MARGARET *looks through the clothes in
the holdall.*)

MARGARET. I've been to Mothercare. Got some of
those new disposable nappies, like you said. Quite different from when you were a baby. (*Sees another carrier, goes
to pick it up.*) What about this bag – what a sweet – won't
she want this dress with the rabbit on?

JACKIE. Leave those! – Things she's grown out of.

MARGARET. Why did you have to try! All by yourself?
Didn't you believe me?

JACKIE. I wanted to see if our theories worked . . .
(*Pause.*) But when I came back from hospital everyone had
cleared out. You'd think I had VD, not a new baby.

MARGARET. He should be here with you, your – (*Stuck
for word.*) – Rosie's father. – You in these flats . . .

JACKIE (*calm*). Mummy, I told you. He visits; and sends money. It was my decision.

MARGARET. Yes but you had no idea! I told you, I told you! Nothing, for nearly three months, nothing, since the day she was born, then a phone call, out of the blue, the potatoes boiled dry!

JACKIE. You knew I'd phone, one day. (*Slight pause.*)

MARGARET. Look at you now, a year ago you had everything, you were so excited about the art school, new friends, doing so well –

JACKIE (*angry*). I'll go back! Yes I will, finish the degree, I won't fail both things! Only think about her at night, her cheek against mine, soft and furry, like an apricot . . .

(ROSIE *makes a snuffling noise in her sleep.*)

JACKIE. . . . She'll be happy, won't she? . . .

MARGARET. After you phoned . . . after you asked us . . . Daddy went upstairs and got your old high chair down from the attic. (*Pause.*) Like sisters, he said. A new little sister . . . (*Bends down to* ROSIE.) Aren't you, precious?

JACKIE (*panics*). Mummy – she's got to know – I can't come and visit, with her not knowing. I can't!

MARGARET. Jackie, darling, we can't go over this again – you know as well as I do it would be impossible –

JACKIE. I don't believe you!

MARGARET. When she's grown up, you can tell her; when she's sixteen.

JACKIE. It'll be too late!

(*Silence.*)

Give me back the bags.

MARGARET (*gently*). You've got such opportunities.

JACKIE. Expectations.

MARGARET. Yes!

JACKIE. Yours.

MARGARET. You've got to –

JACKIE. Why? (*Pulls away holdall.*) Why not just Rosie?
MARGARET. You've got to go further than me – and Rosie too. (*Quietly.*) Otherwise . . . what's it been worth?
JACKIE (*pause*). Here, take them. (*Gives* MARGARET *the bags.*) You haven't told Granny and Grandad?
MARGARET. Not yet. I'll talk to them. (*Tentative.*) – Perhaps you could stay with them, just till Christmas, while you find a new flat? . . . (*Bends to* ROSIE.) My little lamb . . . What's this?
JACKIE. She has to have a red sock to go to sleep.
MARGARET. You keep one.
JACKIE (*puts one sock in her pocket*). Love her for me . . .
(MARGARET *picks up the Moses basket.*)
JACKIE. I'll help you to the car.
MARGARET. It's all right, Daddy will be there.
(MARGARET *picks up the bags. As she goes to the door.*)
JACKIE. I'll come for Christmas. And visit, lots. (*Pause.*) Whenever I can afford the fare to London.
(MARGARET *exits.*)
JACKIE (*calls after them*). Sing to her at bathtime, especially the rabbit song . . . (*Silence. Pause. She picks up the bag she told* MARGARET *to leave. As she pulls out the clothes, she is suddenly hysterically happy. She holds up the rabbit dress.*) – Wore this the day you first smiled, you wouldn't let go of my hair, – do you remember?! (*Holds up another.*) – And your first bonnet . . . (*Gentle.*) And the shawl . . . wrapped you up, like a parcel, the day we left hospital; all the way back in a taxi, bringing you home . . . (*Pause.*) Our secrets, Rosie. I'll take care of them. (*Pause.*) You'll never call me 'Mummy'. (*Silence. Screams.*) Rosie! Come back! – Mummy, Mummy!
(*Blackout. For a moment in the darkness, the sound of a baby crying. In a dim light we see* MARGARET *rocking a bundle. She comforts the baby with the following words, until the baby quietens and coos:*)

142

MARGARET. There now, there now hush! Did you have a nasty dream? My precious. Mummy's here now. Mummy's here, Rosie. There now . . . Did you have a bad dream, Jackie? It's all right. Ssh . . . ssh . . .

(*As the lights come up bright for the next scene,* MARGARET *turns and billows out the sheet which was forming the bundle.*)

COMMENTARY: This play confronts the potent dilemma of how to juggle the demands of a career with those of raising a child. Notice that this scene takes place in Jackie's flat; this is her territory and yet her mother has never been here before. How does this affect the way both women behave and react to one another? Margaret still treats Jackie like a child, do you think this is justified? Jackie is at a crucial point in her life where she is forced to make a radical and irrevocable choice. She opts to pursue her career – do you think she made the right choice? The two women are overwhelmed with mixed emotions and awkward tension; neither is sure that this is really the best solution, but given the options it seems the only way out. On one thing at least they are both in agreement, that Jackie should pursue her opportunities and career to the full. To Margaret, Jackie is still her daughter, her baby, and she treats her in a slightly condescending way. Notice that Margaret's very first words to Jackie are critical and nagging in tone; in everything she says there is an implicit reproach. How does this affect Jackie who so desperately wants her mother's approval? It is their relationship that dominates their conversation; it takes them both quite a time to focus on Rosie. Jackie is in a susceptible impasse: she both wants to be mothered and to be independent.

A Perfect Ganesh
Terrence McNally

Act 1, scene 4. A hotel room with an overhead fan and a balcony. India. Now. Or very recently.

Margaret Civil (50s) is married to Alan and has two grown children. Katharine Brynne (50s) is married to George, has two children and some grandchildren. These two women from Connecticut have been best friends for years. They decide to take a trip together to India, breaking the tradition of their shared family holidays. Both of them have lost their firstborn sons: Katharine's gay son, Walter, was horribly murdered three years ago and Margaret's four-year-old son, Gabriel, was killed in a hit-and-run accident; but she has kept this a secret from everyone, including Katharine. Both women carry a heavy burden of suffering and despair: Katharine still grieving for Walter and Margaret terrified by a lump she has found in her breast; this too she is keeping a secret. There is no evidence that either of them have ever worked, but they are articulate and educated 'home makers'. Katharine who is 'something of an enthusiast' is drawn to self-help groups and has just completed a course on 'Nurturing your Inner Child'. Margaret by contrast says of herself, 'Everyone thinks I'm a bossy bitch.' As this scene starts they are settling into their hotel room, following their long eighteen-hour flight from New York. Their Indian guide has just left the room and Katharine has thanked him for all his help with the Spanish phrase 'Muchas gracias'.

MARGARET. Really, Katharine!
KATHARINE. What?
MARGARET. That is so patronizing!
KATHARINE. What is?
MARGARET. Speaking Spanish to an Indian. What is that? Your generic Third World 'thank you'?

KATHARINE. I'm sorry, but I don't know the word for 'thank you' in Hindi.

MARGARET. Well, it isn't *gracias*!

KATHARINE. He knew what I meant.

MARGARET. He would have known what you meant in your native language. *Gracias* reduces him to the level of a peon and you to that of a horrid tourist.

KATHARINE. My intention was to thank him, Margaret. On that level I think my *gracias* was highly effective. Now which bed would you like?

MARGARET. It's really of no interest to me.

KATHARINE. I wish you would adopt such a generous attitude towards me. I'll take this one then. I hope you remembered the alarm clock. That was your responsibility! (*They have begun to unpack.*)

MARGARET. I'm sorry, but if we're going to travel together you've got to understand something about me. I am very sensitive to the feelings of others.

KATHARINE. You could have fooled me.

MARGARET. Frankly, you've said and done several things that have offended me since we got on the plane. No, 'offended' is too strong a word. Let's say 'embarrassed'. There! I've said it and I'm glad. The air is cleared.

KATHARINE. Don't stop now, Margaret, I'm all ears.

MARGARET. You're sure?

KATHARINE. Absolutely! If we're going to 'travel together' for the next two weeks, let's have absolute candor. I hate that outfit.

MARGARET. Be serious! That remark about Jewish food just now. I could have died. Comparing one of their gods to a bagel.

KATHARINE. He compared him to a bagel. I only said he sounded like something Jewish you ate.

MARGARET. Will you keep your voice down?

KATHARINE. No! And stop saying that. I am sick and

tired of being told to keep my voice down when I am not in the wrong. And even if I were in the wrong, you have no business telling me to keep my voice down. I am not your cowed daughter or your catatonic husband and I am not about to become your cowed and catatonic traveling companion. I'm me. You're you. Respect the difference or go home. I came to India to have an adventure. This is not an adventure. This is the same old Shinola.

MARGARET. Well it's nice to know what your best friend really thinks of you. And your family.

KATHARINE. I didn't mean that. I'm very fond of Joy. And Alan's just quiet around us. I'm sure he's quite talkative when you two are alone.

MARGARET. Not especially.

KATHARINE. I'll give you 'O for a Muse of fire'. I probably do it just to annoy you, like you and the Lalique.

MARGARET. Every time you say it, I say to myself 'O for someone who didn't say "O for a Muse of fire" at the drop of a hat.'

KATHARINE. It wouldn't bother me if you did.

MARGARET. Well that's the difference between us.

KATHARINE. If you can't respect it, at least observe it.

MARGARET. You've changed. Ever since you went to those lectures in Bridgeport. Nurturing your Inner Child! You know what I say? Stifle him! If we all nurtured our inner child, Katharine, this planet would come to a grinding halt while we all had a good cry.

KATHARINE. Well maybe it should. (*There is a pause. They are each lost in their own particular thoughts. When they take a breath and sigh, it will be together.*)

MARGARET. 'O for a Muse of fire' is right! Bartender! One fiery Muse, a decent analyst and an extra-dry gin martini.

KATHARINE. Don't say that. I think it's wonderful what you've done. I couldn't have done it.

146

MARGARET. I finally know what the skin of your teeth means. It's a layer you don't want to be involved with. Anyway, I'm sorry I let it get under my skin. Not you, 'it'.

KATHARINE. It's Shakespeare. 'Muse of fire.'

MARGARET. I know that. That is so patronizing to tell me it's Shakespeare!

KATHARINE. I didn't know it until they showed it on Public Television. It's the first line of *Henry V*. How hard it is to really describe anything. And I have that trouble, don't you?

MARGARET. I don't know. Probably.

KATHARINE. 'Muse of Fire' is my talisman. It's my way of telling myself 'Savor this moment, Katharine Brynne *nee* Mitchell. Relish it. It is important. You'll never be here or feel this way again.'

MARGARET. This is what I mean. Those lectures in Bridgeport.

KATHARINE. That's not nurturing my Inner Child. It's Shakespeare. Telling you you can be a pain in the ass is nurturing my Inner Child.

MARGARET. Now I'm a pain in the ass! (*They have finished unpacking and will now begin to make ready for bed.*)

KATHARINE. I didn't say you were a pain in the ass. I said you could be a pain in the ass. I'm hoping the next two weeks you won't be. (*The phone begins to ring. This time* MARGARET *will answer it.*)

MARGARET. I have never been a pain in the ass for two more weeks. Have I? (*Into phone.*) Hello?

KATHARINE. That's right, we were only in Barbados for 11 days.

MARGARET. Blame that trip on Barbados, not me! Hello?

KATHARINE. Everyone's toilet was broken.

MARGARET. Seven years later she throws Barbados in

my face! Hello? (*She hangs up.*) There's no one there.

KATHARINE. I hope you haven't come to India for their telephones *or* the plumbing!

MARGARET. There you go again! Patronizing! I've come to India for personal reasons. Just as you've come for yours.

KATHARINE. I thought we came to India for a vacation.

MARGARET. I adore you, Kitty, even when you're impossible.

KATHARINE. No, you don't. I don't think we are best friends. I don't think we know each other at all.

MARGARET. I'm sorry you feel that way. I feel very warmly towards you.

KATHARINE. I know. Me, too.

MARGARET. It's going to be fine. From this moment on, we're going to get along famously and become the very best of friends.

KATHARINE. Who says?

MARGARET. My Inner Child. Do you mind if I nip in the loo first?

KATHARINE. Where do you think we are, luv, the Dorchester? (MARGARET *goes into the bathroom area of their hotel room.*) We have a balcony. Did you know we had a balcony? We have two of them! (*She steps forward onto the balcony.*)

MARGARET. How does the rest of it go? Do you know? 'O, for a Muse of fire' *what*? (KATHARINE *stands looking at the harbor in front of the hotel. She is overwhelmed by what she sees.*)

KATHARINE. 'O, for a Muse of fire, that would ascend The brightest heaven of invention!'

(MARGARET *screams in the bathroom.*)

MARGARET. Don't mind me. It's only a waterbug the size of a standard poodle.

KATHARINE. 'A kingdom for a stage, princes to act,
And monarchs to behold the swelling scene!'
Well something like that.

COMMENTARY: For the first time in years Katharine and
Margaret are free to travel by themselves, and yet they are still
encumbered with the emotional baggage of family life. They are
travelling to India on a kind of pilgrimage: they each have their
'personal reasons' and secret agendas. They believe that this trip
to India will help them relieve the suffering they have secretly
endured over the years. The strains of travelling together are
already becoming apparent in this scene. The close proximity
and the alien surroundings test their friendship. They respond
to the world in quite different ways. Katharine embraces
experience with an effusive theatrical relish, whereas Margaret
is much more uptight, cautious and conventional in her
responses. Notice how they behave like a tetchy married couple,
irritating and provoking one another.

Serving it Up
David Eldridge

Act 1, scene 3. A park in east London. The 1990s.

Wendy (late teens) works in a hairdressing salon which she hates –
'My whole life revolves around washing hair for one-fifty an hour.'
She always aspired to be a secretary but never got the right grades.
She and Teresa (late teens) have been best friends since primary
school days.

(WENDY *and* TERESA *sit on the park bench. They both*
smoke.)
WENDY. I've given up on a real tan. (*A beat.*) I've got to
get on me mum's sunbed, Trese.
TERESA. You don't need it. Sunbed just gives you
wrinkles.
WENDY. White legs. Look at them, Trese – like a milk
bottle!
TERESA. Get some tanning lotion.
WENDY. It goes all streaky.
TERESA. Your legs are all right.
WENDY. This country. Sun – we've had sun all summer
and the week I'm off for a weekend on the beach it's been
pissing down. (*A beat.*) Mary's not coming any more.
Fucking bitch. She's not getting her deposit back.
TERESA. What are you going to do?
WENDY. Well, you're not doing anything this weekend.
TERESA. I can't afford it, Wend.
WENDY. Come on – what do you reckon?
TERESA. I don't know.

WENDY. It'll be a laugh.

TERESA. A caravan in Bognor?

WENDY. You're just a snob.

TERESA. I'm not. I just draw the line at Bognor, that's all. (*A beat.*)

WENDY. Well, if you're not going to go I'll just have to pull tonight.

TERESA. Where are we going?

WENDY. Don't know.

TERESA. I'm not going to the Red Fox again.

WENDY. Options?

TERESA. I'd rather get food poisoning at the Red Fox.

WENDY. They've changed the music now, Trese . . .

TERESA. My idea of a night out does not involve five hundred sixteen-year-olds bobbing up and down on their first fucking E.

WENDY. They don't play hardcore any more.

TERESA. What is it? Load of metallers and a trip-head shagging a weirdo in the corner?

WENDY. I thought you liked Indie?

TERESA. Will you just leave it, Wend.

WENDY. Sorry!

TERESA. Look, there is more to life than a Friday night and a weekend in Bognor, right.

WENDY. Why don't you just leave the PMT routine, Trese. (*Pause.*)

TERESA. I'm a week late.

WENDY. I thought you stopped seeing Freddie?

TERESA. Yeah – well.

WENDY. Forget it, darling. Talk to me about it in a week's time and you'll wonder what you were worrying about. (*A beat.*) Tell you what. Wouldn't mind a dirty weekend with that Nick.

TERESA. You're a nympho!

(*They laugh.*)

Nick's all right. His mate Sonny's a prat though.
(*Pause.*)

WENDY. I used to fancy Sonny.

TERESA. He looks like an ape.

WENDY. He's not that bad.

TERESA. Sonny's just like the other blokes round here. If you want to meet someone decent you've got to look up west.

WENDY. I haven't got West End money.

TERESA. And most of them are wankers. I met this city bloke once, Wend. Honestly – he stroked his mobile like it was his prick. And I said to him – I don't care where you're from or how much money you've got, if you try and touch my tits again I'll knee you in the bollocks –
(*Pause.*)
I don't know why you bother with blokes so much.

WENDY. You're just a feminist.

TERESA. I'm not a feminist!

WENDY. You are! Always saying it about men. Next thing you'll be shaving your head and shagging a lesbo.

TERESA. Bloody cheek. I don't just let blokes take liberties with me.

WENDY. I like a bloke who takes a few liberties. At least it's a bit of excitement.

TERESA. It's not. They crap all over you. I'm not getting married.

WENDY (*nodding somewhere in the audience*). Look at him over there walking his dog. I bet he ain't a piss-taker.

TERESA. He must be thirty-odd.

WENDY. I wouldn't mind an older man. Someone to look out for you. Someone to listen to, talk to.

TERESA. No. Look at his face. I've seen that look before. My dad had it. I bet he's just been with a bird, and not his wife either . . .

152

WENDY. No! Not him – he looks like Richard Gere.

TERESA. He's a shit – just like the rest.

WENDY. He's lovely in *Pretty Woman*. Anyway, Cindy Crawford wouldn't go with a bastard.

TERESA. They split up, you silly tart.

(*Pause.*)

WENDY. What will you do then? You can't live on your own . . .

TERESA. I'm not going to live under the thumb.

WENDY. What about when you fall in love?

TERESA. No way!

WENDY. I believe in love.

TERESA. You still believe in Father Christmas.

(*Pause.*)

It's all rubbish, Wend. You'll wake up one morning and think – I'm forty, I'm fourteen stone and I don't know what I'm doing. But before it pisses you off, you look at your old man and you ask him for a cuddle. What does he do? He rolls over, farts, and tells you to go and make him a cup of tea. I don't want that.

WENDY. You've got to have love. You've got to have love, Teresa.

(*Pause.*)

I've been in love – I know what it's like. I was in love with Jason.

TERESA. Jason?

(TERESA *laughs*.)

WENDY. Yes.

TERESA. That plonker? You could hit him with a hammer and that fuckwit would still grin.

WENDY. He had a nice smile.

TERESA. He was born with that. His mum dropped him on his head.

WENDY. Don't take the piss.

TERESA. And he had a twitch. We used to call him Shakin' Stevens at school!

WENDY. You always take the piss.

TERESA. Bloody hell. That's your romance? What was that? Hand up your skirt and make your fanny wet?

WENDY. Fuck off.

TERESA. Wend . . .

(WENDY *goes to leave.*)

TERESA. No, wait. Please, Wendy.

(WENDY *stops and turns.*)

TERESA. You know what I believe, Wend? Sometimes I can see it when I'm here at the park. I look at the kids with their mums and dads, and I know that I shouldn't feel it, because I look at the faces of the mums and they're so heavy and drawn – But I look at the kids and there I see it – life.

(*Pause.*)

This place, the park, the playground – You remember Wend, when we were kids, on the swings. Swinging higher and higher, faster and faster, so you could almost feel, you could jump off and you would fly – but you don't. You hold on tight. We lop off each year backwards and forwards on that swing, and it gets slower and slower and when you finally want to jump – you really want to jump – you're going nowhere, you're stuck.

(*Pause.*)

I'm not saying I'm going to fly, but I can't be tied to a bloke who doesn't give a shit and I can't be tied here for the rest of my life.

WENDY. Are you saying you're leaving?

TERESA. No, no – but I have to be free. I have to have a choice when something comes along.

WENDY. What's coming along? What's going to turn up round here?

COMMENTARY: This play depicts a world of bleak frustrations and dead-end options. Wendy thinks she is streetwise, savvy and sexy, but, as Teresa remarks, she is merely a hopeless romantic. They both intuitively know that they want something better than their current lot, but they can't quite articulate what it is or how they will get it. In this scene Wendy is most concerned with getting Teresa to come away with her for the weekend so that they can have a good time and find some blokes. Teresa, who has an extremely cynical view of the opposite sex and life in general, is reluctant to go along with her. It is interesting to note that it is Teresa and not good-time Wendy who thinks she's pregnant.

Sweet Panic
Stephen Poliakoff

Act 2, scene 3. Clare's consulting room, north London. A rainy late afternoon.

Clare and Mrs Trevel are both in their late thirties. Clare is a single, childless child psychiatrist who has been treating George, Mrs Trevel's eleven-year-old son. George has been bunking off school and his hugely over-protective and ambitious mother is concerned at his generally poor level of achievement when he does attend school. Clare has the ill-luck to be out of town with her partner, Martin, and crucially out of reach when George goes missing while staying with a friend in the country. Although he is found safe and sound, Mrs Trevel becomes unreasonably irate that Clare could not be contacted for the duration of this emotional episode. Her irrational indignation transforms Mrs Trevel into a blend of avenger and stalker who persistently turns up unannounced vowing to wreak professional ruin on Clare. So far Clare's day has been frenzied; she has met up at Marble Arch with her star patient who attacks her, causing her to miss Martin delivering 'the most significant address of his career'. In this scene, Clare has just walked back to her office in the rain. Once through the door she is confronted by Martin who demands that she 'deals' with the troublesome Mrs Trevel who has been waiting all afternoon to see her. As Martin leaves, this scene begins with Mrs Trevel entering Clare's office.

(MRS TREVEL *enters.*)
MRS TREVEL. Ready for me?
(*Slight pause.*)
CLARE. I think so . . .
MRS TREVEL (*laughs*). Nearly said something else, didn't you? (*Watching* CLARE.)

You missed his lecture, your partner. How did that happen?

CLARE. I had some unexpected business to attend to.

MRS TREVEL. I see. (*Lights cigarette.*) Right now, what's the agenda? – Get rid of the crazy lady? For good. Is that right?

(CLARE *looks up startled.*)

MRS TREVEL (*smiles*). You should be able to do that . . . easy.

[(GINA *enters with file.*)

GINA. George Trevel's file.

CLARE (*surprised*). Gina, thank you – before I'd even asked for it!

GINA. Mrs Trevel suggested you might need it.

CLARE. Right. (GINA *moving to go.*) No word from Jess?

GINA. No. (*She exits.*)

(CLARE *with George's file in front of her, opens it.*)]

CLARE. So . . . you want something from here? One piece of paper – and you'll be satisfied?

MRS TREVEL. Yes.

CLARE. Does that include this? – (*Holding up one sheet.*) Your son's birthday, height, weight and school?

MRS TREVEL. Maybe you could look just a little further.

(*Watching her carefully.*)

Are you allowed to use the word freaky?

CLARE (*looking up startled*). What?

MRS TREVEL. I had a young nanny looking after George, everything was, (*She mimics.*) 'That's Freaky!' I supposed in *your* job, you're not allowed to comment all the time 'That's really freaky!' – Not very scientific.

(*Smiles, reaching in her bag.*)

Anyway I'm just warning you, you may find this really freaky . . .

CLARE. And what is in there?

MRS TREVEL. Aha, the other file – *My* File. Don't look like that! (*She laughs.*) What's the ex-index compiler up to now?

(*She produces piece of paper.*)

This is simple – you know broadsheet newspapers often run a series of articles from members of the public, 'The Worst Time of My Life' – that sort of thing? Well, there is a new series – 'The Worst Experience with My Child'. And *I've* done one – about you and I. And my entry has been accepted. (*She lays it down in front of her.*)

And it appears on Monday.

(CLARE *facing her.*)

CLARE. Is that a very wise thing to do, Mrs Trevel? Have you had a lawyer look at it?

MRS TREVEL. All Names are Changed of course, as they say.

(*Opening sheet of paper.*)

But here *you* are.

(*She looks up.*)

Who goes first? (*Without waiting for a reply.*) Me? OK . . . 'The first time I saw her, a handsome confident woman, polite but formidable, and so very much in control – one of the most self-possessed people I've ever met.'

(MRS TREVEL *looks at* CLARE.)

CLARE (*calmly*). But she made you feel extremely lucky to be allowed time with her – even though you were paying for it. Is that what it says? Just guessing.

MRS TREVEL. I'm afraid it's not quite as tame as that. 'A fatal mixture of complacency and arrogance' – that's what it says down here!

(*She looks up at* CLARE.)

'As I moved nearer to her I realise we're about the same age. Soon I work out we're both grammar school girls, both from lower-middle-class families, though of course *she* assumes I'm from a much posher background – both growing up in unfashionable parts of London, glorious Acton and Hendon respectively.' I like that bit . . .

'We probably both had our first sexual experiences about the same time – maybe even shared the same taste in boyfriends, tall gangling types, certainly we liked the same music . . .'

(*Slight pause.*)

'*Now we couldn't be more different.*'

(*She looks up.*)

What does yours say?

CLARE (*watching her very closely*). It's not as colourful, I'm afraid, it's cold and factual.

MRS TREVEL. Cold is good.

CLARE (*staring at file*). 'George's mother is very determined to get results . . . highly motivated for her child.'

MRS TREVEL. I love that, 'highly motivated'.

CLARE. 'Her previous employment shows up in a habit of amassed random pieces of information.' (MRS TREVEL *clucking in agreement.*) 'But currently she is unemployed, her main focus very much her home life –'

MRS TREVEL (*suddenly very animated*). Why don't you say Housewife. I want to be that – officially. I'm proud to be an 'Ordinary Housewife', it's such a great phrase. You should dare to call me that. OK!

(*Slight pause.*)

CLARE (*giving her a couple of pages*). Here, have those. (*As* MRS TREVEL *looks at them.*) Mrs Trevel, did you write this article, and get it published, purely *for this moment*, so you can have a kind of 'duel'?

MRS TREVEL (*calmly*). Yes. Do you want some fruit? (*She produces some peaches from her bag. Amused smile, glancing at pages.*) You're right, this is bland, isn't it? (*She looks up.*) And mine of course is going to appear in *print*, in black and white.

(*Perfectly calm.*)

You mustn't forget what my real purpose is in all this. It's *what happens to you* – remember?

(*Eating fruit for a moment.*)

Now shall we get to the really gritty bits?

'SHE is unmistakably a product of late sixties/early seventies liberalism . . .' No, this isn't it . . . here!

'Despite all her poise – and while paying lip service to the worries of a middle-class mum like myself – she can't disguise her basic *contempt*. It is masked, of course, but I can see it.'

'Her real passion is reserved solely for those poor children, the NHS cases she deals with, those lost disadvantaged souls. She approaches what she's doing for *me* as purely a form of car maintenance – just tuning up the kids. Something that has to be endured, to pay for her real work.'

(*Pause. CLARE moves around stage taking cigarette out of MRS TREVEL's packet.*)

CLARE. That is ridiculous and simplistic.

I could say, quite calmly, I refute it. But in fact it's utter shit, *total shit* and that's what it should be called.

(*Momentary pause. MRS TREVEL watching.*)

I clearly wouldn't survive a week in my practice if people thought that about me.

I do not make those judgements.

(*She moves over to cupboard in wall, begins to produce a series of Jess's models, both small ones and medium ones.*)

But there's something much more important that you're wrong about. Far more important *to me*.

(*She tugs at cigarette for a moment, the models in a pile at her feet.*)

MRS TREVEL. I didn't know you smoked.

CLARE. I don't smoke.

(*She blows smoke.*)

I see children – all the time –

MRS TREVEL. Of course. I know –

CLARE. – from all sorts of backgrounds. The children of famous novelists and members of the SAS, children of taxi drivers, of traffic wardens with their peculiar new uniforms, and one kid whose father is a pest controller.

(*She moves.*)

I have to get to know them, and especially their inner worlds. Have to be able to enter their imaginations – see the world through their eyes . . .

And what you said is *totally untrue*. It's garbage.

MRS TREVEL. Which particular piece of garbage of mine did you have in mind?

CLARE. The story about George – when he asked you, 'Am I being targeted correctly, Mummy, towards the right market?' That is *not* how kids see themselves, or see the world now, none of them, not even your son. They do not feel there's such a *rush*.

That is an adult fantasy – a myth.

MRS TREVEL. That's what you're calling it?

CLARE. *Yes*. Just like that other myth – that KIDS CAN'T CONCENTRATE any more, only for a couple of minutes at a time, because of TV, MTV, computer games . . . everything has to be images, and flicking channels, that is *such a lie* too!

MRS TREVEL. You *want* to believe it's a lie –

CLARE. *No* – that is not what I find. From the kids. It's not what happens here. And yet it gets recycled again and again – 'books will be dead within five years' – it's absolute crap.

MRS TREVEL (*smoking*). So I'm recycling myths, am I?

CLARE. Kids' imaginations are just as vivid, just as anarchic, as ever, maybe more. (*Indicating models.*) Look at these, the work of a thirteen-year-old girl.

(*She stands them up across stage.*)

She started with a fragment of the Houses of Parliament,

then she moved on to this great version of the Albert Hall! . . . a sort of super biscuit tin, whose top rolls off – with these strange rather sinister black lozenges inside – Christ knows what those are meant to be!

The whole city is here – though there's a particular bias towards South Kensington for some reason!

Harrods oozing as you can see . . . a very spiky, dangerous Albert Memorial . . .

(MRS TREVEL *moving among models*.)

Just think of the amount of time and concentration that's gone into these! Hours and hours, to create her vision of the city.

MRS TREVEL. They're great. Strange . . . but great. You should open it to the public, a model city on your roof! (*She looks up*.) You must find her a really interesting case.

CLARE. Yes she is, I'll admit that. She does all this work for me, but she will do nothing at school.

MRS TREVEL. This is Jess?

CLARE. Yes.

MRS TREVEL. The one you're waiting to hear from? I can see why.

(*She kneels down centre stage, among the models, to look at them more closely*.)

They're haunting – a sort of two-finger salute, a fuck-you sign, to anybody who looks at them. (CLARE *turning in surprise*.) And here's the American influence . . . how we half embrace it and half hate it. And they all look uninhabited, don't they?

(*Picks one up*.)

Is this what's happening to the city? Nobody knows what the centre of cities will look like, do they? – when everybody's work patterns change.

Somebody said, on the radio, 'Oh, the inner cities will be

regenerated by the Entertainment Industry!' What crap that is!

CLARE. Yes, that is.

MRS TREVEL. I'd like to keep one of these, a very small one, maybe Battersea Power Station. (*She is kneeling among them.*) God preserve me, from *my* children being too *original*.

CLARE. What? (*Sharp.*) What did you say?

MRS TREVEL. I said, don't let my children be too original please – they'll never succeed.

CLARE. You really think that?

MRS TREVEL. Yes.

CLARE. That's a startling thing to say . . . (*Slight pause.*) Never heard somebody say that.

(MRS TREVEL *gets up.*)

MRS TREVEL. It's really raining now . . . (*Suddenly turning.*) Do I get to hear my child's recording – what he said here?

CLARE. No, you do not.

MRS TREVEL. So there *is a* recording? Of George?

CLARE. Maybe.

MRS TREVEL (*watching* CLARE). What happened at Marble Arch? Something happened to stop you getting to the lecture?

CLARE. A boy, who used to come here, got overexcited.

MRS TREVEL. He attacked you?

(*Pause.*)

CLARE. No, not attacked, no. That's overstating it. He got upset.

MRS TREVEL. Was it that beautiful boy who's always waiting to see you?

CLARE. I'm not commenting on that.

MRS TREVEL. It obviously was.

CLARE. I told you –

MRS TREVEL. It must have been unpleasant, whoever

163

the boy was. Suddenly all this bile coming out – was it bile? It must have been a shock. (*Slight pause.*) Come on, you can tell me – before they come in . . . Did he bruise you? (*Taking her arm to look,* CLARE *flinching.*) Jesus . . . ! You're really hurt.

CLARE (*obviously in pain*). No. It's nothing. (*Slight smile.*) You get very used to kids hurling abuse at you in this job. It happens quite a lot.

(*Quiet.*) I just wanted . . . I suspected this individual was not as happy as he made out . . . but I wanted him to be . . . I wanted to be proved wrong.

(*Pause.*)

But it was OK. I'm fine . . .

MRS TREVEL. You walked across London in the rain. Even though you were late for everything! And you say it's OK?

CLARE. Yes. What's more my car was parked right underneath where we were, right below, and yet I walked all the way back.

That must seem a little odd, I admit.

(*Slight pause.* CLARE *has turned away.*)

MRS TREVEL. I'll take you back there. To where your car is. I'll give you a lift.

CLARE. No. That's not necessary.

MRS TREVEL. Oh yes, it's easy for me. On my way. We'll go there together.

CLARE. Thank you, but no –

MRS TREVEL. I think you should come.

CLARE. You can have this. (*Handing rest of file.*) The whole file – I really don't see why not now.

(MRS TREVEL *takes file, but doesn't bother to look at it.*)

CLARE. Have you got what you wanted?

MRS TREVEL. No. You were right – it's not going to be of any interest to me. (*Looking across.*) That's why you should come.

COMMENTARY: This play is concerned with the past; how it affects our capacity to understand and control what happens to us now and in the future. Mrs Trevel projects her obsessive sense of paranoia and failure onto Clare herself. Her son's problems become secondary to her own neuroses. Mrs Trevel, who dubs herself the 'mother from hell', projects an uptight preciosity and genteel menace. She is brimming with nervous ingenuity and energy. To anyone who encounters her she is both disoriented and disorientating. In this scene the audience is seeing Clare through Mrs Trevel's eyes. Both women are on edge: Mrs Trevel has been waiting anxiously all afternoon for this confrontation and Clare has been bedeviled by one encounter after another. How does this affect the way they interact? Their confrontation is like a 'duel' of nerves waged with language. Both tormentor and tormented are highly articulate. Notice how the stage directions indicate the two women are constantly watching each other, interrogating with their eyes. Clare tries to maintain a professional distance from Mrs Trevel, but her patience starts wearing thin. She is obviously caught off-guard by the splenetic venom of Mrs Trevel's attack. For both actors it is vital to pace this scene very carefully and not play it on a single frenetic note.

Talking in Tongues
Winsome Pinnock

Act I, scene I. A house in London. A room with lots of coats in it. There is the constant sound of party music outside. Late evening.

Claudette (20s) is a 'young black woman' like her close friend Curly (20s). They are ambitious, articulate, professional working women who have known each other since school days. They have come to a New Year's Eve party together. As this scene starts Claudette has 'hurt her feet. She sits down and takes her shoes and tights off, examines her foot. Curly enters.'

CURLY. Why did you run off like that?

CLAUDETTE. My foot.

CURLY. I thought there was something wrong with you.

CLAUDETTE. There is. He trod on my toe. He's crushed it. It's hanging off on its cord, look.

CURLY. Calm down and let Curly have a look at it. It can't be that bad.

CLAUDETTE. Trust me to get caught in the stampede . . .

CURLY. A man stands on your toe –

CLAUDETTE. One minute I see all their heads turn toward me, next thing I know I'm flat on my back with footmarks all over me.

CURLY. It was an accident.

CLAUDETTE. It's always the same when a white woman comes in the room.

CURLY. Don't start, Claudette.

CLAUDETTE. Our men are straining at the leash like hunting dogs on the scent of the fox. Ow. Careful.

CURLY. There's only two black men here. That's hardly a pack of hounds, is it? Anyway, Bentley's a good bloke.

CLAUDETTE. Why do you think they invited us here? Do you think it's to get the party going? We're supposed to be good for a party, aren't we?

CURLY. Leela invited us.

CLAUDETTE. So why did they invite Leela?

CURLY. Because they're friends of Bentley's.

CLAUDETTE. Hours we've been here and we're the only ones dancing.

CURLY. The fun won't start till after midnight, then you'll think you're in a madhouse.

CLAUDETTE. It takes these people a long time to warm up.

CURLY. Stop complaining. Least you got asked to dance.

CLAUDETTE. While he's dancing with me he's looking over my shoulder at her. I might as well be a burst blow-up rubber doll he's dragging around.

CURLY. We can always dance with each other.

CLAUDETTE. What is it with our men?

CURLY. I read a good book about it. I'll lend it to you.

CLAUDETTE. I don't give a toss about the science of it. What I want to know is where the next fuck's coming from.

CURLY. Sit still or this'll hurt.

CLAUDETTE. Careful. One man told me he thought black women were too aggressive.

CURLY. I'm not aggressive.

CLAUDETTE. Aggressive my arse. Pride. That's what it is.

CURLY. People do sometimes fall in love, Claudette.

CLAUDETTE. What do they feel when they're holding her? Have you watched their faces when they're holding a

167

white woman? They look as though they're in a seventh heaven. Makes you feel like the invisible woman. It's not as if you can escape from it. She's everywhere you go. And every blown-up picture of her diminishes us.

CURLY. For God's sake, Claudette, sit still.

CLAUDETTE. It's not as if they want to be your friend. The only time one of them wants your friendship is when she's trying to get her hands on one of our men, and once she's done that they're both off without a backward glance: she never rated us in the first place and he doesn't want to be reminded of the detritus he left behind on his way to the top.

CURLY. Stand up.

(CLAUDETTE *stands.*)

CURLY. Does it still hurt?

(CLAUDETTE *practises putting weight on the injured foot.*)

CURLY. Can you walk on it?

(CLAUDETTE *walks up and down.*)

CLAUDETTE. What I really hate is the way they have to get off the tube before you do, as though you were some maid following on behind. Or they'll sit beside you brushing their hair out like Rapunzel, thinking they're making you jealous. Many's the time I've missed my stop because I've had my mouth full of some white woman's hair.

CURLY. We're supposed to be welcoming in the New Year, not griping about the one just gone.

CLAUDETTE. Touchy.

CURLY. It's the same old record, Claudette, every time we meet. I don't blame Leela for not coming out with us any more.

CLAUDETTE. What's she been saying?

CURLY. Nothing.

CLAUDETTE. She's been talking to you about me.

CURLY. I told you. She hasn't said a word. (*Slight pause.*)

I used to like Friday nights. It was fun, wasn't it? Giggling at the pictures, getting drunk and having a good bitch. I haven't had a good bitch for ages. Why don't we start Friday nights again?

CLAUDETTE. Friday nights have been cancelled due to lack of interest. Times I've left messages and neither you or Leela got back to me. God knows what you've been up to, and as for Leela, well you only have to look in her eyes to see she's too far gone for intelligent conversation.

CURLY. I'm happy for her.

CLAUDETTE. So am I. I'm also just a bit concerned. Did you see the look in Bentley's eye when he caught sight of the living Barbie doll?

CURLY. Leave them alone, Claudette. They're doing all right.

CLAUDETTE. She's flying high as a kite all right. Basking in this aura of cosy coupleness. She hasn't got time for us any more.

CURLY. You two used to be such good friends.

CLAUDETTE. If you've been single more than six months, coupled women shun you, as though singleness were some kind of curse.

CURLY. You'd be the same. I know I would.

CLAUDETTE. She's high on love all right. I want to be there when she comes crashing down.

CURLY. You sound as though you might enjoy it.

CLAUDETTE. I didn't mean it like that.

CURLY. I wonder about you sometimes. I can't see why you have to be so angry all the time.

CLAUDETTE. But then you wouldn't, would you?

CURLY. What does that mean?

CLAUDETTE. Nothing.

CURLY. Starting on me now, are you?

CLAUDETTE. Should I start on you?

CURLY. What gives you the right to tell people how to live?

CLAUDETTE. When did I tell anyone how to live?

CURLY (*referring to* CLAUDETTE*'s foot*). That should be all right now, as long as you don't stand in the way of any rampant male egos. (*Starts to go.*)

CLAUDETTE. Where you going, Curly?

CURLY. I fancy a dance and a drink.

CLAUDETTE. You know how you get after a few drinks.

CURLY. What's wrong with forgetting myself for a while?

CLAUDETTE. Me, I don't want to forget, I want to remember.

CURLY. See you outside then.

CLAUDETTE. What's up, Curly?

CURLY. Nothing.

CLAUDETTE. I've known you long enough to know when something's wrong. Why don't you tell your Auntie Claudette?

CURLY. I can't.

CLAUDETTE. I'm not such a heartless bitch, am I? Come on, Curls, you know how I feel about my friends. Is it that white guy?

CURLY (*nods*). It finished. (*Slight pause.*) It was just one of those things. Happens to everyone, doesn't it? It was nobody's fault. I mean, we got on well enough. We got on really well. He even took me to meet his parents.

CLAUDETTE. He must have liked you, Curls, if he took you to meet his parents.

CURLY. Nice people. Very simple life, you know the type. Nice. When we got there, they'd bought me a present. They'd bought me this expensive make-up set. Mirror, brushes, eye-shadows, lipstick, the lot.

CLAUDETTE. You don't wear it much, do you?

CURLY. Just as well because it was the English rose collection, wasn't it? English rose they were expecting.

CLAUDETTE. Guess who's coming to dinner.

CURLY. We're all just standing there. He's saying nothing. They're saying nothing. I'm holding the English rose collection, not knowing whether to laugh or cry. Then we had dinner. (*Slight pause.*) You're thinking it serves me right, aren't you? You're thinking I'm always setting myself up to get hurt like this.

CLAUDETTE. It's not your fault, Curls.

CURLY. You've got to keep trying, haven't you? Why didn't he tell them?

CLAUDETTE. You're too good for him.

CURLY. It wouldn't have happened to you.

CLAUDETTE. Fuck that. Let's dance. I thought we were supposed to be welcoming in the New Year, not whingeing about the old one. Come on, Curls, my feet are itching.

(CURLY *stands*.)

CLAUDETTE. Teach them how to dance, eh?

(*They go.*)

COMMENTARY: In this play Winsome Pinnock wanted to explore 'whether relationships can, in fact, be politicised. Claudette is a fanatic when it comes to expounding her particular brand of racial politics, which are based on a form of separatism, the belief that interracial relationships are a betrayal of the community and, more seriously, a betrayal of the black woman which is connected to her historical degradation. However, Claudette's fanaticism is an attempt to avoid her own pain and longing caused by the traditional double oppression both within and outside their communities that some black women experience.' Although Claudette is a 'fanatic' it is important that you find a sympathetic chord to temper her more strident outbursts otherwise you risk losing the audience's interest. Although

Curly is by comparison calmer and more sanguine you must find the dynamic in her personality so that she is not merely a foil to her friend. Later in the play Curly turns on her friend with these words, 'She is right, though, isn't she? Claudette always is . . . The shouting's got to stop some time. Why can't we just live together, why can't we just have some peace?' Remember that they're at a party, they've been drinking and dancing, and may be a little the worse for wear.

Weldon Rising
Phyllis Nagy

Tilly and Jaye's apartment on Little West 12 Street in New York City's meat-packing district. It is the hottest evening of the year.

Tilly and Jaye (both not quite 30) are lesbian lovers. Tilly is 'older than she'd like to be. Pretty enough, which is problematic for her. Naturally curious and incongruously romantic.' Jaye is 'very fit, clean and thoroughly gorgeous. Mean, caustic and not afraid of being unsympathetic. Not at all coy or girlish, but not butch either.' They are both from middle-class backgrounds. They first met in an accidental encounter at Kennedy Airport and have been together ever since. They live in a state of hermetic lethargy, subsisting on the beer they steal from supermarkets. Their apartment (which 'should not be represented naturalistically') is strewn with empty beer bottles. From the window of this apartment they have just witnessed 'a horrible crime', the vicious murder of a gay man. They observed passively and did nothing to help the dying man, except to call the police. As this scene begins they have been watching what is happening in a nearby apartment between a gay man and a transvestite; Tilly is particularly fascinated by the goings-on.

TILLY. Men are violent. Even when they wear dresses. Let's stay home forever.
(JAYE *kisses the back of* TILLY's *neck while* TILLY *continues to observe the unseen scene.*)
JAYE. Hold still and let me bite your neck.
TILLY. It's too fucking hot for that. Do we have any more beer? I drink too much beer.
JAYE. You don't drink enough. You're coherent when you're drunk.

TILLY. It's a hundred and twenty degrees and if I don't have another beer I'm gonna . . . ouch. Stop that. You're hurting me.

JAYE. When you're drunk, you let me bite your neck.

TILLY. You know, he's really very skinny. But he has a nice ass. WOULD YOU PLEASE STOP MAULING ME.

JAYE. Sorry. No more beer. We're dry.

TILLY. Liar. You're hoarding it. Under the floorboards.

JAYE. Tough. No sex, no booze.

TILLY. I can't believe you're doing this to me. It's blackmail.

JAYE. Hey. These are the rules. I bite your neck, you get a beer. I rip off your clothes, you get another beer.

TILLY. Don't be such a boy.

JAYE. Listen to yourself. Since when did you decide to be celibate?

TILLY. Since it's gotten so hot I can't think straight. Jesus. I need a drink. Please.

JAYE. Bulldyke.

TILLY. Flattery just won't work any more, honey. Look. That silly drag queen is washing his pantyhose.

JAYE. You've been at that window for weeks. Talk to me, Tilly.

TILLY. I wonder what size he wears. I hate my name. It's withered. We got any more popcorn?

JAYE. Pay some attention to me or I'll get another girlfriend.

TILLY. I bet he wears queen-sized. Long legs. Yeah. Well. Who are you kidding? Nobody else would have you. You're a mess.

JAYE. Fuck off.

TILLY. No, really. You're worse than me. And you got no booze in the house, no food and you got no air-conditioning. Why don't we have air-conditioning?

JAYE. I like the heat. It's unpleasant.

TILLY. And why does this skinny little fuck keep packing and unpacking clothes? I mean, why doesn't he just trash them?

JAYE. I'm out of here.

TILLY. Oh yeah? Where you going?

JAYE. I told you. I'm on the prowl.

TILLY. I hate it when you're pathetic.

JAYE. Okay. So I might be persuaded to stay home and hook you up to a beer i.v.

TILLY. Don't go out.

JAYE. Why not? I look good under lampposts. Cheap and sexy. That's me.

TILLY. You might lose your keys. Then what. Then you'd be lost to the streets.

(JAYE *turns* TILLY *towards her.*)

JAYE. You ought to get out, too. Come with me.

TILLY. I can't. My hair's dirty. I smell.

JAYE. Tilly. It's all right to go outside now. It's all over.

TILLY. We should have helped him. We should have run out into the street then.

JAYE. I'm not listening to this any more.

TILLY. Why didn't we help him? Now look at him. Nearly naked and still trying to hide his bald spot.

(JAYE *holds out a beer to* TILLY, *as if from nowhere.*)

JAYE. Whoops. Look what I found. It's a . . . Corona.

TILLY. I knew you were holding out on me. Bitch. Give it here.

JAYE. Fuck me first.

TILLY. Were you always this mean?

JAYE. Yup. Now. What's it gonna be?

TILLY. We used to be civilised, you know.

JAYE. Too late for that. I'll count to ten. One. Two.

TILLY. I can't help this, Jaye. I can't. We watched a man die and I can't move now. I want to sit at the window and rot. And drink till I drop.

JAYE. Three. Four. I swear, when I get to ten, this all goes down the drain. Five. Six.

TILLY. For chrissakes. Just let me have the fucking beer, all right?

JAYE. Seven. Eight.

TILLY. Okay. OKAY. STOP. What do you want? I'll do it.

JAYE. On your knees.

(TILLY *drops to her knees*. JAYE *goes to her, opens the beer*.)

JAYE. Mouth open, head tilted back.

(TILLY *complies*. JAYE *feeds beer to* TILLY.)

JAYE. We did what we could. We called the cops. We're not responsible.

TILLY. Just . . . shut up and feed me.

(JAYE *bends to kiss* TILLY.)

JAYE. What do you love more: me or booze?

TILLY. Shut up. Feed me.

(JAYE *kisses* TILLY.)

COMMENTARY: Phyllis Nagy's apocalyptic play depicts the soulless poverty of urban life. The play raises challenging questions about sexual identity, guilt, cowardice, self-preservation and indifference. The abbreviated dislocated scenes reveal the characters' different reactions and responses to a senselessly horrific murder. The actors in this scene must be bold and confident in dealing with the overt sexuality of the stylised dialogue. 'Much of the punctuation used in the play is not standard and intended to create a non-naturalistic pattern to the language. The play works best in performance when strict attention is paid to the specifics of the punctuation. Similarly, the use of capitals in some lines does not necessarily indicate an increase in volume; rather it is meant to indicate shifts in thought.' The playwright offers the actors no information on the characters' personalities or backgrounds. It is important to find ways to physicalise the sense of the oppressive heat in the tightly claustrophobic apartment.

The Woman Who Cooked Her Husband
Debbie Isitt

Scene 5. Hilary and Kenneth's house somewhere near Liverpool, England.

Hilary (40s) is married to Kenneth, an ageing Teddy boy. 'She is dressed in a green taffeta outfit, green tights and shoes. She wears her hair in a beehive.' She is an expert cook and homemaker. After nineteen years of marriage, Kenneth starts to have a secret affair with Laura (20s–30s). Laura, who enjoys her freedom and having a good time, is dressed identically to Hilary. Laura has been pushing Kenneth to leave Hilary, but he wants to wait until the time is 'right'. In the preceding scene Hilary confronts Kenneth with her suspicions that he is having an affair with another woman, which he strenuously denies. Laura's frustration leads her to come to Hilary's house to have a showdown.

HILARY. Hello . . . I know you, don't I, it's . . . don't tell me . . .
LAURA. Laura.
HILARY. Laura, of course it is . . . what can I do for you? How did you know where I live?
LAURA. I've come for a chat.
HILARY. Oh, I suppose Sal told you it's an open house. Boyfriend trouble, is it?
LAURA. Yes it is, as a matter of fact. I don't really know how to tell you – I know you're going to kill me – I don't blame you – he won't tell you – I've begged him and begged him and I can't go on like this . . .
HILARY. Tell me what – who?
LAURA. You probably already know – I mean we met at

one of Sal's parties – he was there – you couldn't make
it . . .

HILARY. What dinner couldn't I make? What are you
talking about? I go to all Sal's do's – she doesn't have a do
if I don't go. Has she sent you about something?

LAURA. I've come to explain.

HILARY. Explain what?

LAURA. Why your husband's been so distant . . . Where
he's been, what he's been up to.

HILARY. You what?

LAURA. He's been with me.

HILARY. Is this a joke, love – only I've got something
burning under the grill . . .

LAURA. I just thought you ought to know.

HILARY. I don't know what you're talking about.

LAURA. I'm sorry.

HILARY. Yes, well, I'm sorry – I'm sorry, I can't think
what you're on about. Whatever it is you've come here to
say you'd better say it then piss off, I'm busy.

LAURA. Kenneth and I are lovers, we have been for a
long time – he wouldn't tell you so I have.

(*Pause.*)

HILARY. I'm sorry?

LAURA. I had to tell you.

HILARY. This isn't very funny.

LAURA. I know it isn't funny. I'm sorry, I had to tell you.

HILARY. There's a mistake – you're mixed up, you're
telling lies – I'll tell my husband about you when he comes
in – he won't take this lightly I can tell you . . . If you've
got a grudge against him for something, this is no way to
sort it out . . . I know you're lonely – on your own – but
just because you haven't got a boyfriend you can't go
round making up stories, fantasising about other women's
husbands . . . it was the party, wasn't it – you were looking
at me, jealous – because I had a husband and you didn't.

179

LAURA. I honestly thought you knew ... I mean you must have known something. I suppose you just didn't want to admit it. I think it's best if you do. It is over, your marriage. Kenneth has been planning to leave you for months.

HILARY. I've just about had enough of this ... You come to my house, tell me my marriage is over – who the hell do you think you are? You don't know my marriage, you haven't got a clue what you're talking about – people like you want locking up!

LAURA. It wasn't all my fault – I wasn't looking for anything – it just happened. There must have been something lacking.

HILARY. Is that right? Listen, if you're trying to tell me my husband and I have a crap sex life you're very much mistaken – if you're trying to say my husband's told you we don't make it any more, then you're a liar – even if my husband knew who you were, he'd tell you how much he loved me – and you to get lost – all he needs he gets at home, don't worry about that!

LAURA. He just doesn't fancy you any more.

HILARY. We've been married nearly twenty years – nobody fancies each other after twenty years, love – what the fuck is fancy? We make love because we love each other. Are you thinking of offering him a bit on the side, flattering his ego? Try it, see where it gets you – I mean anyone can do that – it doesn't make you special.

LAURA. I'm special enough that he wants to leave you for me.

HILARY. Leave me? You must be joking – you've completely imagined this whole thing. Kenneth wouldn't go with you if you were the last woman alive. I know his taste. I know him, I'm married to him – he loves this house – but of course you wouldn't know that, seeing as you don't know him ...

180

LAURA. You'll get over it, I know you will.

HILARY. Get out.

LAURA. I'm sorry.

COMMENTARY: This play portrays a high-energy emotional journey. The playwright suggests in her foreword that each character 'has its own route and the action flares when the paths are crossed. Most of the work should be done out of the scene, building up the emotional truth ready to enter the scene so that the actors can just "be" there during the scene . . . The play should be served up at a fast, furious pace with savage emotional input, clear fast thought changes and an innocence that keeps the play alive and real . . . Dialogue exchanged with wit and passion . . . but never completely hiding the pain that runs very deep amongst all three characters.' This is the first time these two women have met. Laura has come at a most inconvenient time for Hilary who is busy in the kitchen and does not want to be disturbed. Laura arrives at Hilary's house and is somewhat disarmed by Hilary's open friendliness. Since Laura is all too aware of Hilary's existence she should have a definite advantage over her rival. She hesitates and stumbles, awkwardly trying to get out what she really wants to say. But Hilary's composure quickly evaporates as she is confronted by her worst nightmare. They both display and try to mask their mutual curiosity, hatred and jealousy. At this point in the play they both define their identity in terms of their relationship to Kenneth. Why do you think the playwright has indicated that the two women are identically dressed and how might this affect your performance? As you will see when you read the play, Kenneth is the unlikely subject of such fierce rivalry and competition.

(NB You can find the continuation of this scene on page 93 of this volume.)

Play Sources

Amy's View by David Hare (Faber)

The Beauty Queen of Leenane by Martin McDonagh (Methuen)

Boys' Life by Howard Korder in *Boys' Life & Search and Destroy* (Methuen)

Broken Glass by Arthur Miller (Methuen)

Closer by Patrick Marber (Methuen)

The Cripple of Inishmaan by Martin McDonagh (Methuen)

Dog Opera by Constance Congdon in *The Actor's Book of Gay and Lesbian Plays* (Penguin)

The Heidi Chronicles by Wendy Wasserstein in *The Heidi Chronicles and Other Plays* (Vintage)

Kindertransport by Diane Samuels (Nick Hern Books)

The Lodger by Simon Burke (Methuen)

Low Level Panic by Clare McIntyre (Nick Hern Books)

The Memory of Water by Shelagh Stephenson (Methuen)

My Mother Said I Never Should by Charlotte Keatley (Methuen)

A Perfect Ganesh by Terrence McNally (Dramatists Play Service)

The Pitchfork Disney by Philip Ridley in *Philip Ridley Plays: 1* (Methuen)

Raised in Captivity by Nicky Silver (TCG)

Serving it Up in *Serving it Up & A Week With Tony* by David Eldridge (Methuen)

Shopping and F***ing by Mark Ravenhill (Methuen)

Simpatico by Sam Shepard in *Sam Shepard Plays: 3* (Methuen)

Some Voices by Joe Penhall (Methuen)

Sweet Panic by Stephen Poliakoff in *Blinded by the Sun & Sweet Panic* (Methuen)

Talking in Tongues by Winsome Pinnock in *Black Plays: 3* (Methuen)

Two by Jim Cartwright in *Jim Cartwright Plays: 1* (Methuen)

Weldon Rising by Phyllis Nagy in *Phyllis Nagy Plays: 1* (Methuen)

The Woman Who Cooked Her Husband by Debbie Isitt (Warner/ Chappell)

Acknowledgements

The editors and publishers gratefully acknowledge permission to reproduce copyright material in this book:
Simon Burke: *The Lodger*. Copyright © 1994 by Simon Burke. Reprinted by permission of Methuen Publishing. Enquiries regarding all performance rights should be addressed to Curtis Brown, 162–168 Regent Street, London WIR 5TB. Jim Cartwright: *Two*. *Two* was first published as *To* in 1991 by Methuen Drama and is reprinted here with corrections. Copyright © 1991, 1994, 1996 by Jim Cartwright. Reprinted by permission of Methuen Publishing. Enquiries regarding all performance rights should be addressed to Judy Daish Associates Ltd, 2 St Charles Place, London WIO 6EG. Constance Congdon: *Dog Opera*. Copyright © 1995 by Constance Congdon. Reprinted by permission of the William Morris Agency, Inc., 1325 Avenue of the Americas, New York, NY 10019. Enquiries regarding amateur performance rights should be addressed to Samuel French Inc., 45 West 25th Street, New York, NY 10010. Enquiries regarding professional performance rights should be addressed to the William Morris Agency, Inc. David Eldridge: *Serving it Up*. First published by the Bush Theatre in 1996. Copyright © 1996, 1997 by David Eldridge. Reprinted by permission of Methuen Publishing. Enquiries regarding all performance rights should be addressed to William Morris Agency, 31/32 Soho Square, London WIV 5DG. David Hare: *Amy's View*. Copyright © 1997 by David Hare. Reprinted by permission of Faber & Faber Ltd. Enquiries regarding all performance rights should be addressed to Casarotto Ramsay, National House, 60–66 Wardour Street, London WIV 4ND. Debbie Isitt: *The Woman Who Cooked Her Husband*. Copyright © 1991, 1993 by Debbie Isitt. Reprinted by permission of

Shepard. Reprinted by permission of Methuen Publishing. Enquiries regarding all performance rights should be addressed to MacNaughton Lord Representation Ltd, 200 Fulham Road London SW10 9PN. Nicky Silver: *Raised in Captivity*. Copyright © 1995 by Nicky Silver. Reprinted by permission of TCG. Enquiries regarding all performance rights should be addressed to George P. Lane, William Morris Agency, Inc., 1325 Avenue of the Americas, New York, NY 10019. Shelagh Stephenson: *The Memory of Water*. Copyright © 1997 by Shelagh Stephenson. Reprinted by permission of Methuen Publishing. Enquiries regarding all performance rights should be addressed to Hamilton Asper, Ground Floor, 24 Hanway Street, London W1P 9DD. Wendy Wasserstein: *The Heidi Chronicles*. Copyright © 1990 by Wendy Wasserstein. Reprinted by permission of Harcourt Brace Jovanovich. Enquiries regarding all performance rights should be addressed to ICM, 40 West 57th Street, New York, NY 10019.

187